I0501943

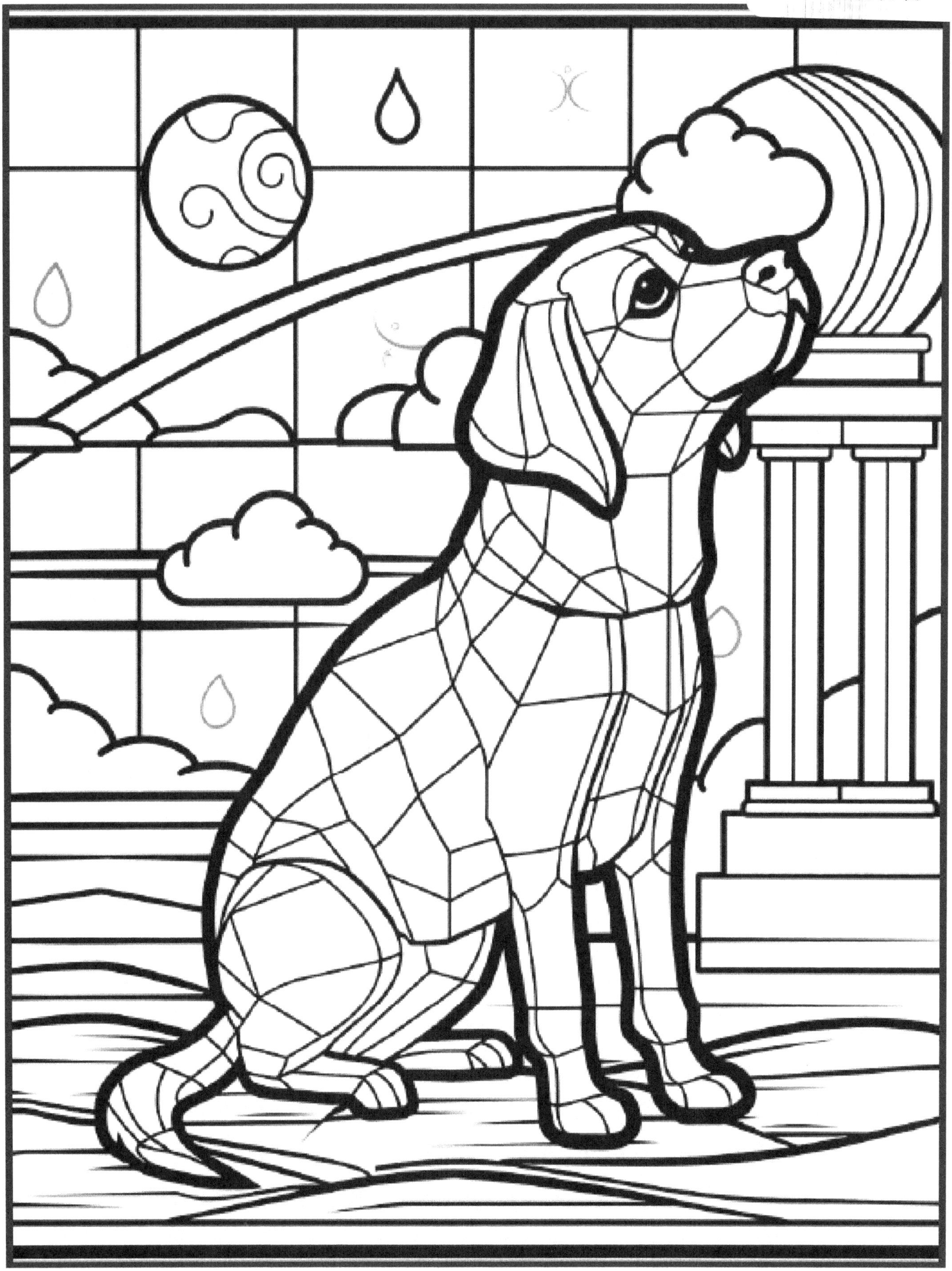

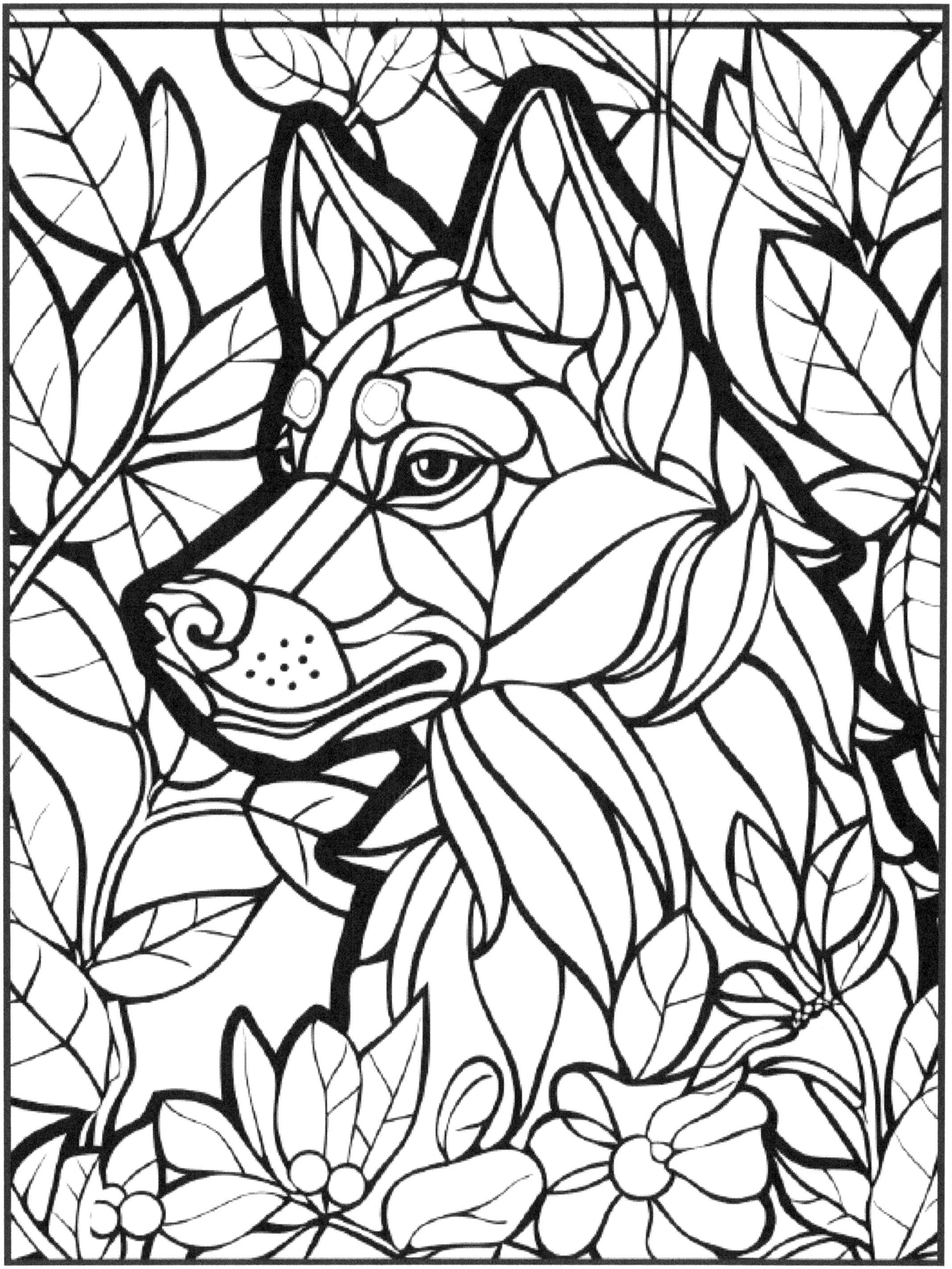

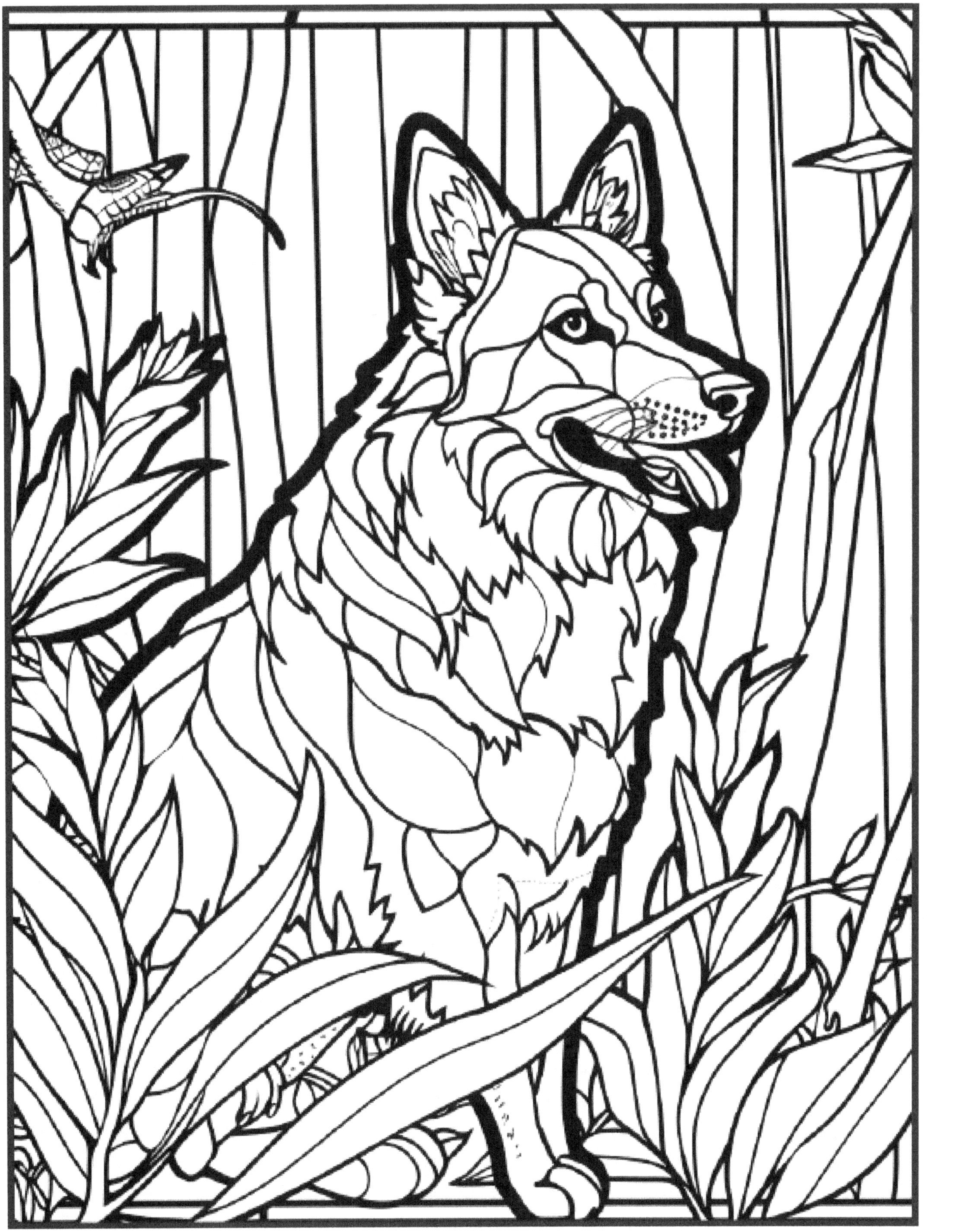

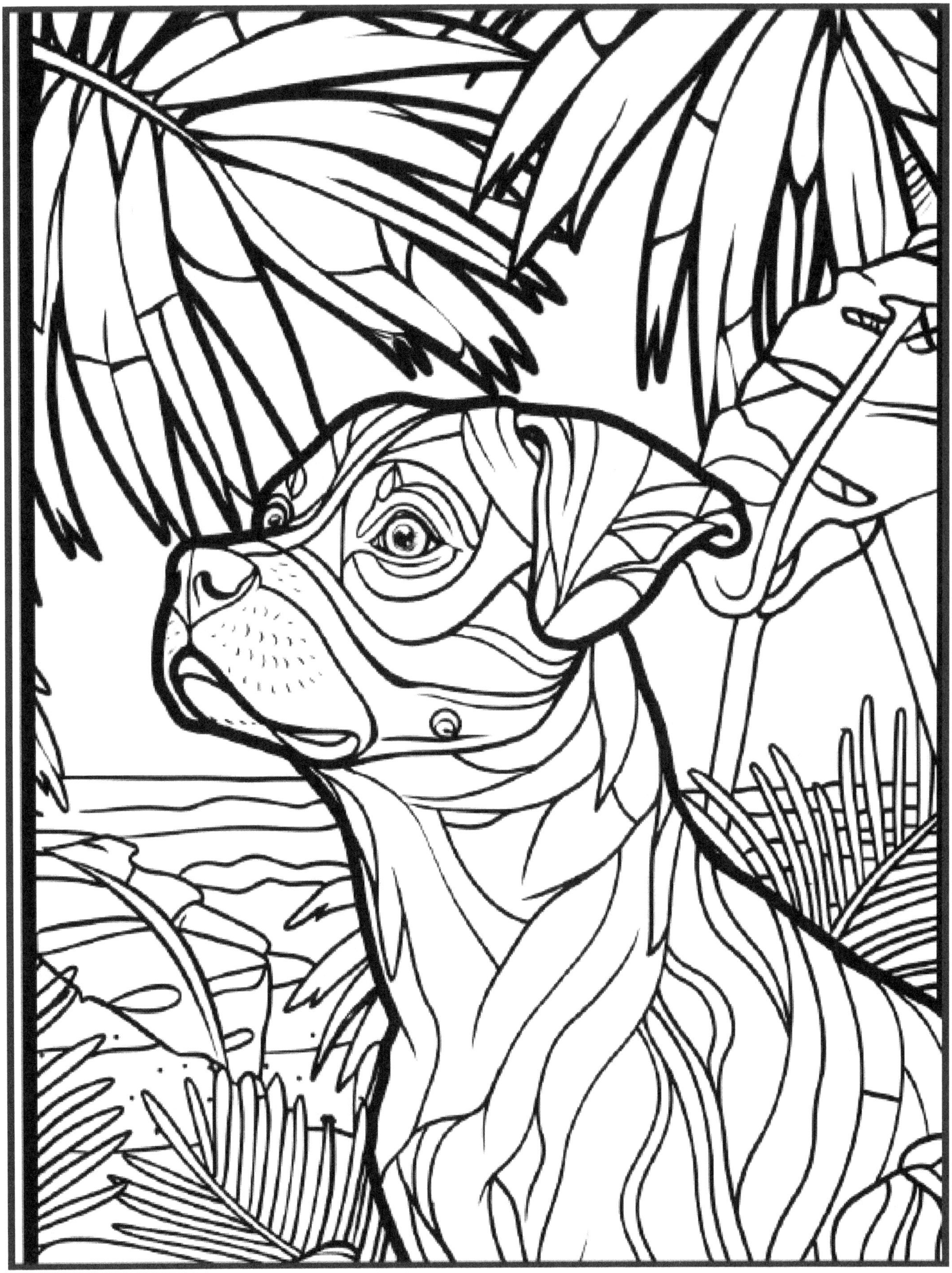

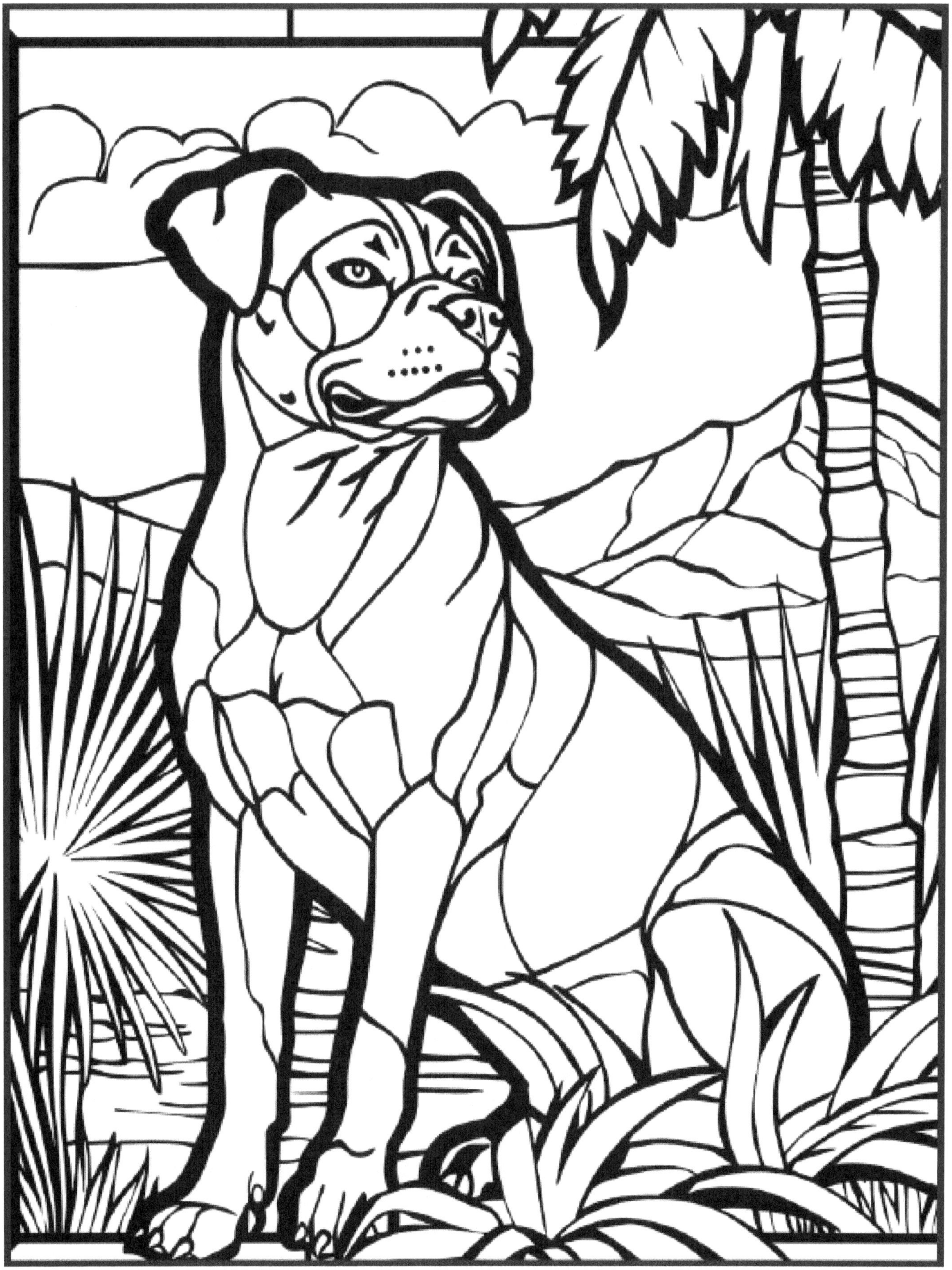

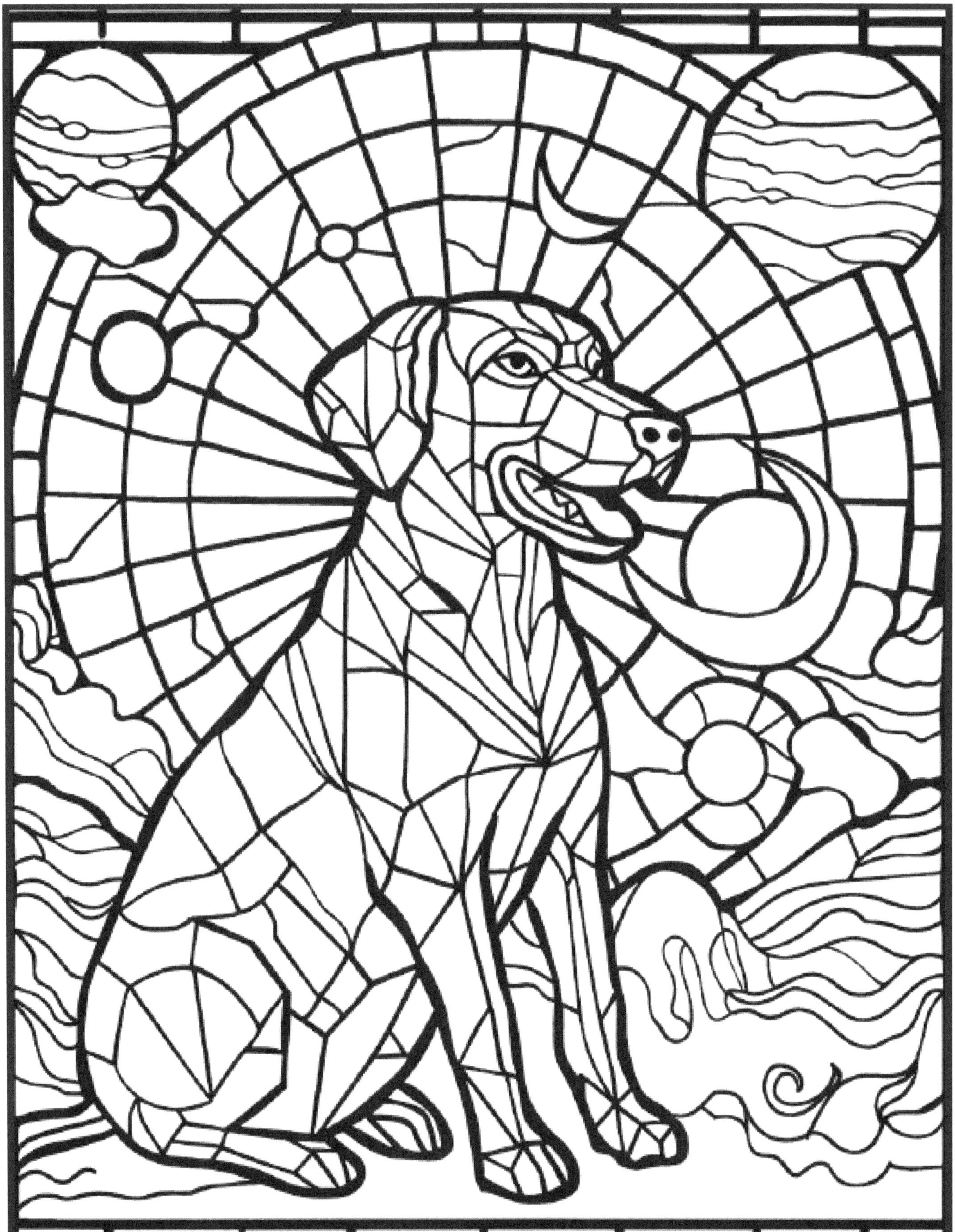

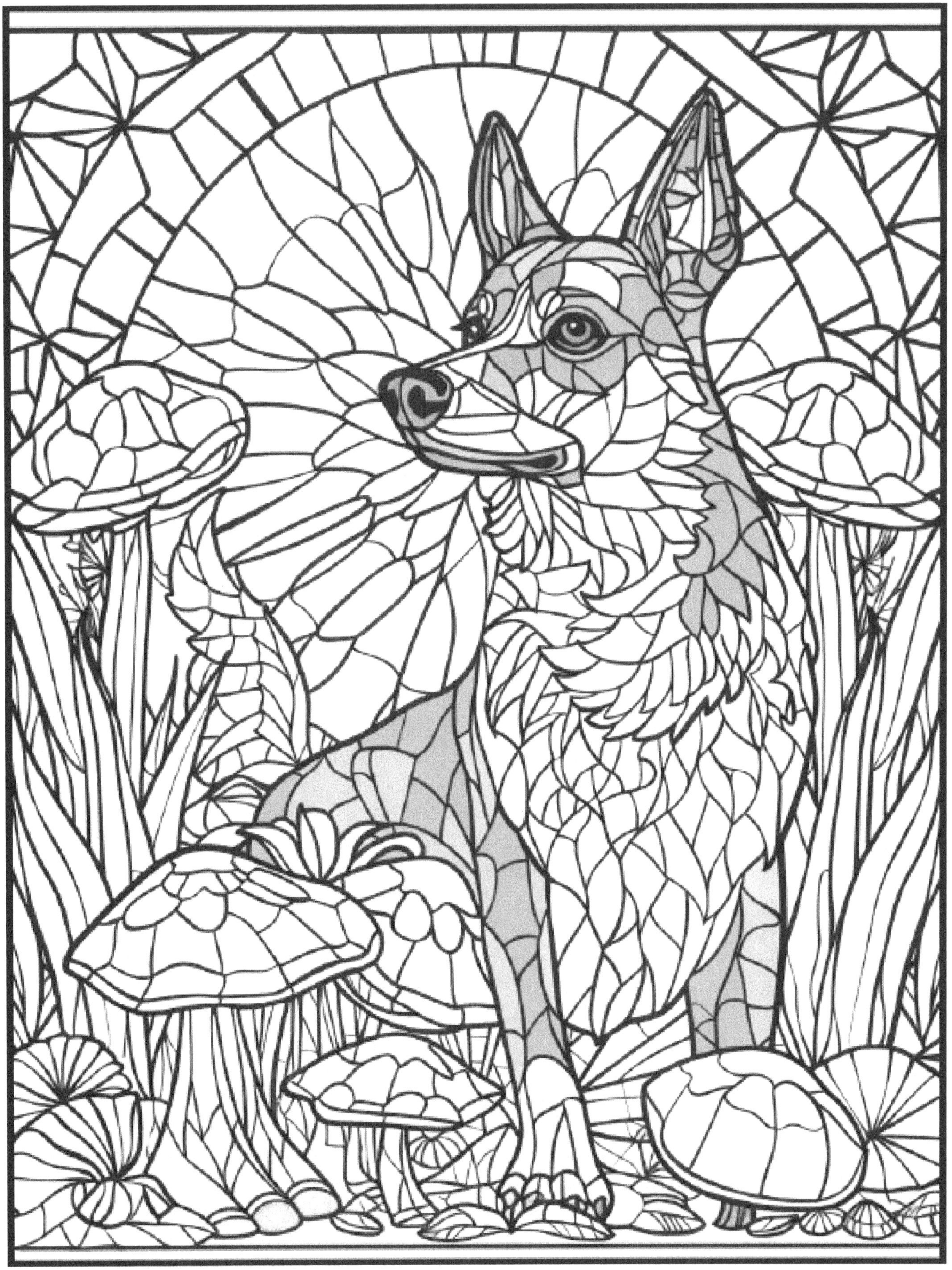

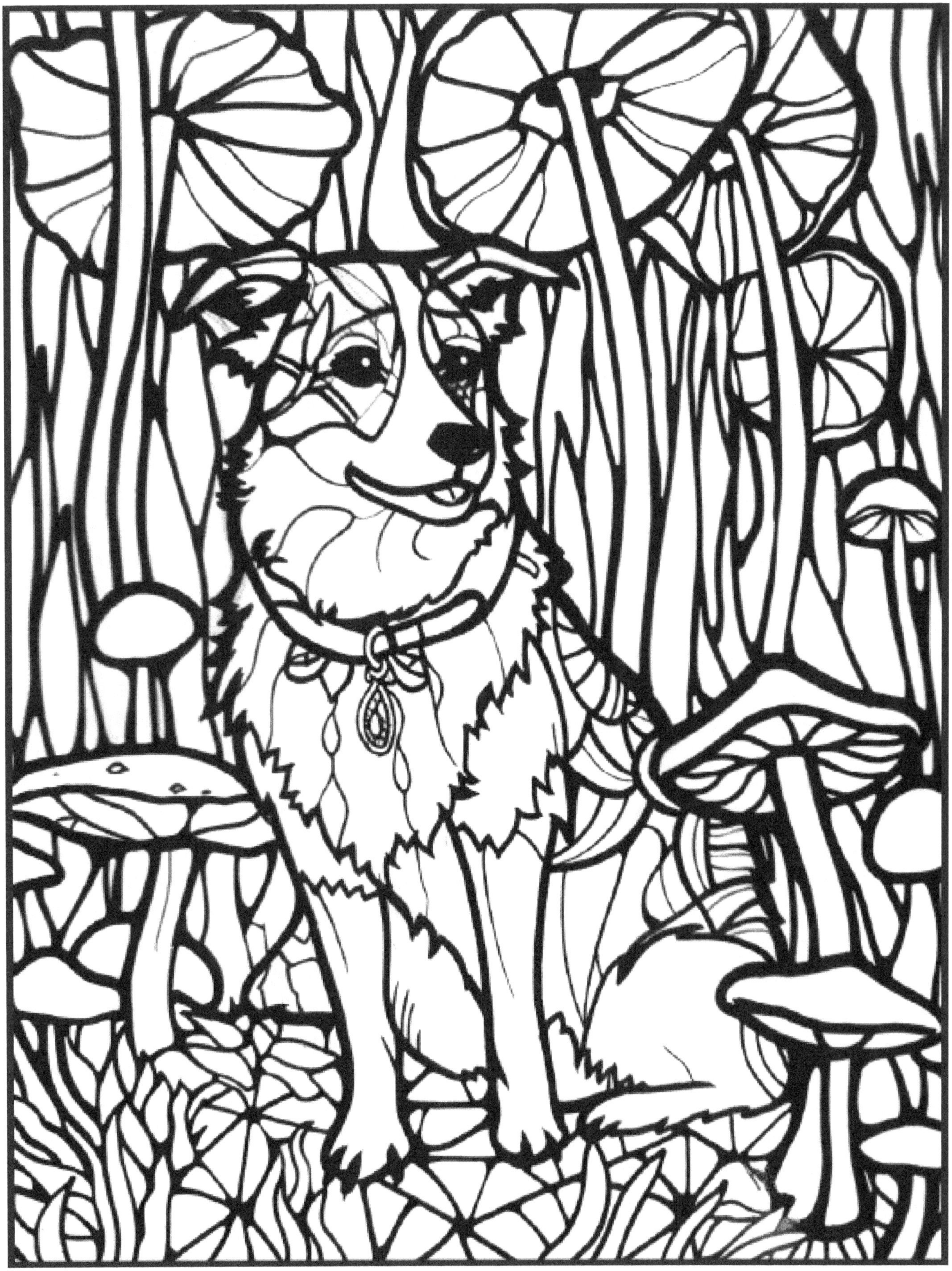

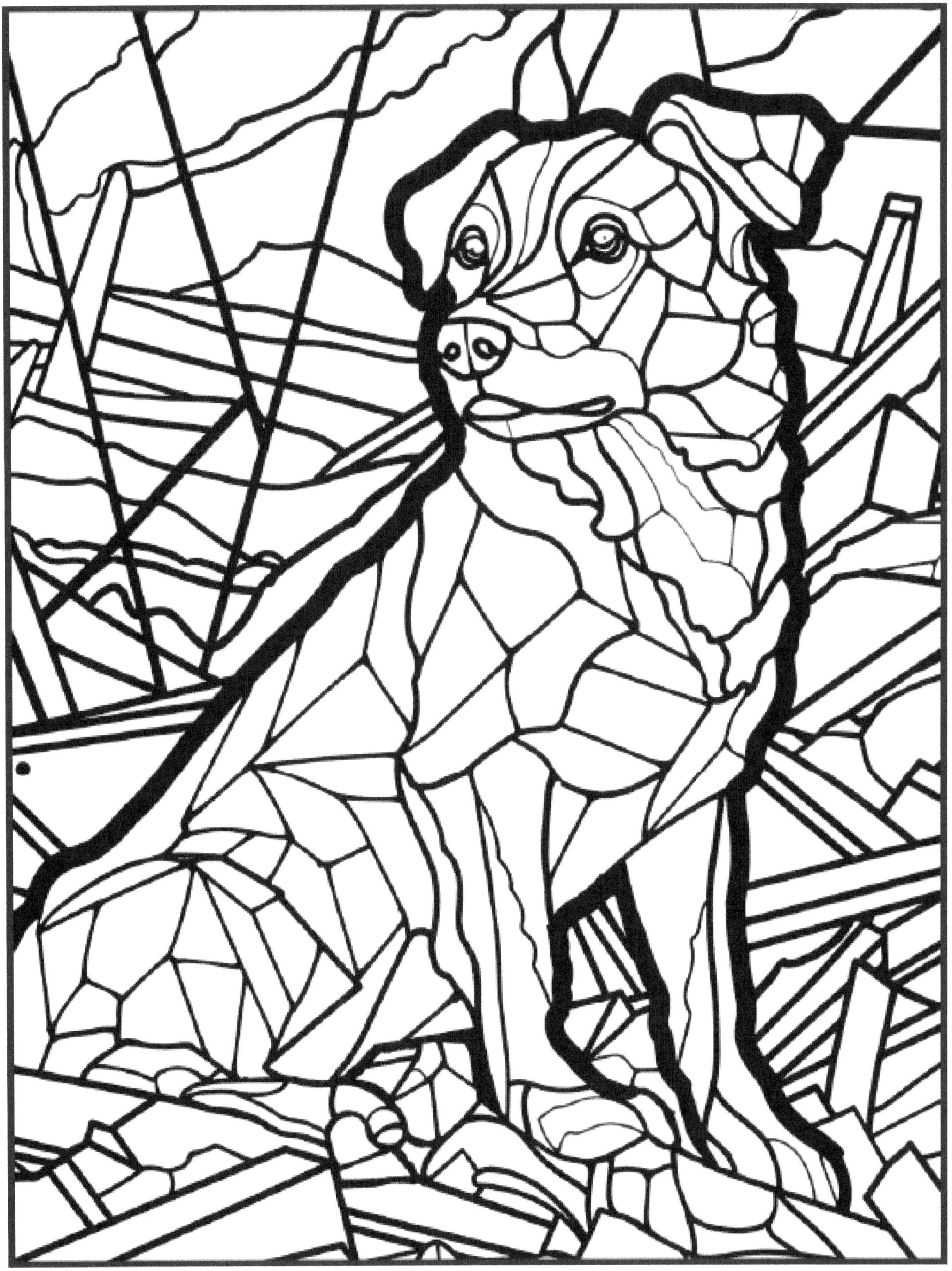

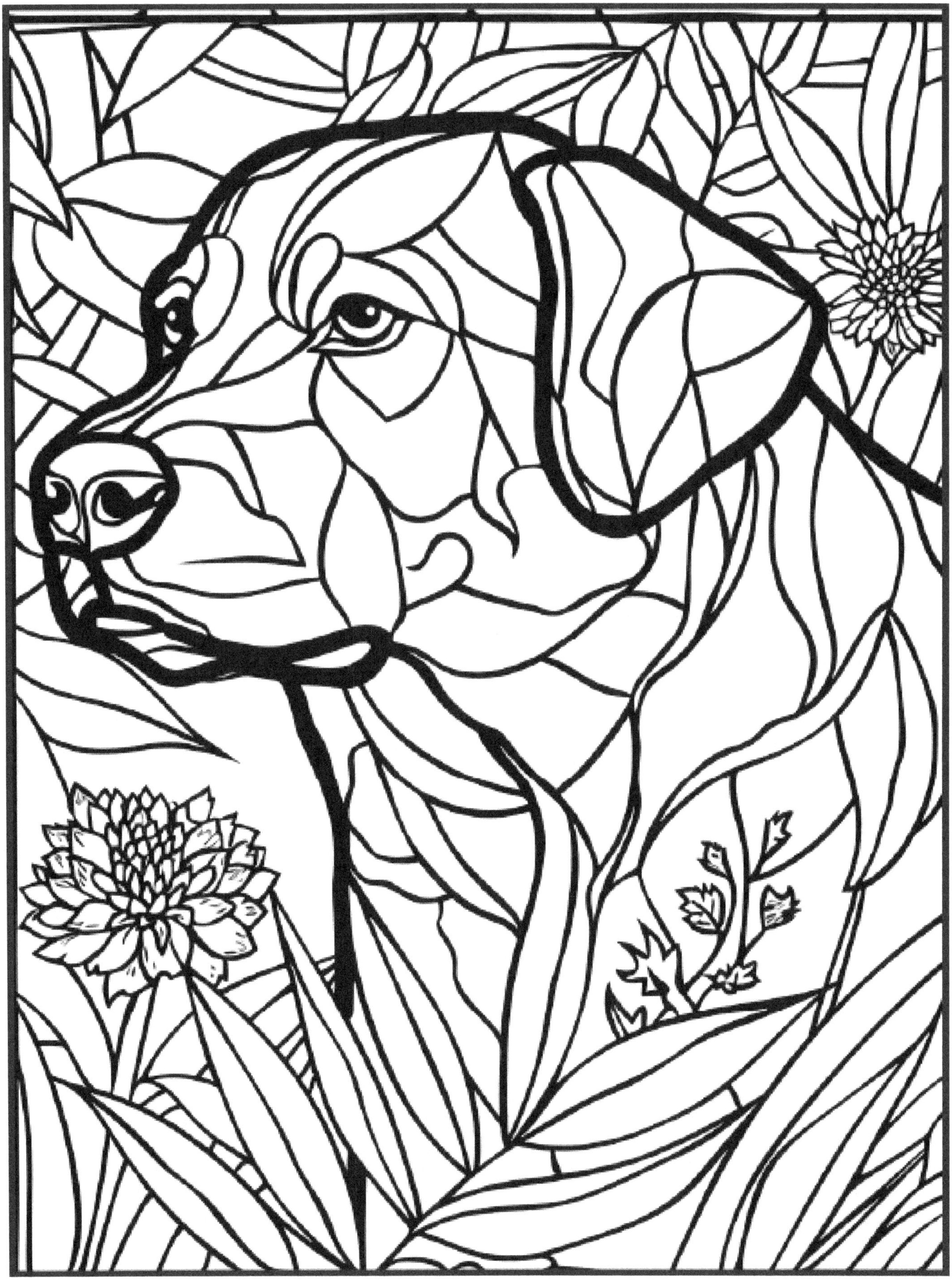

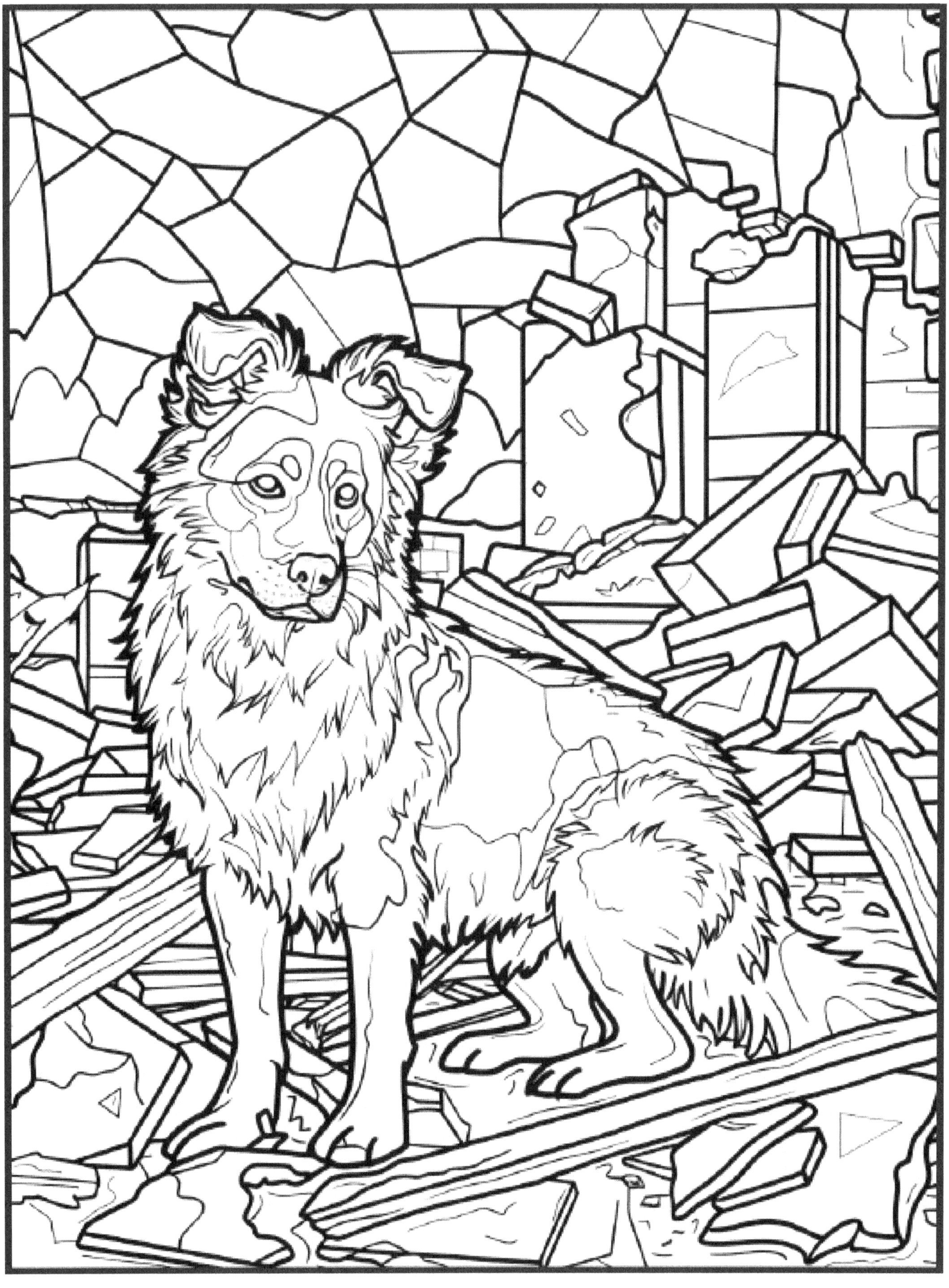

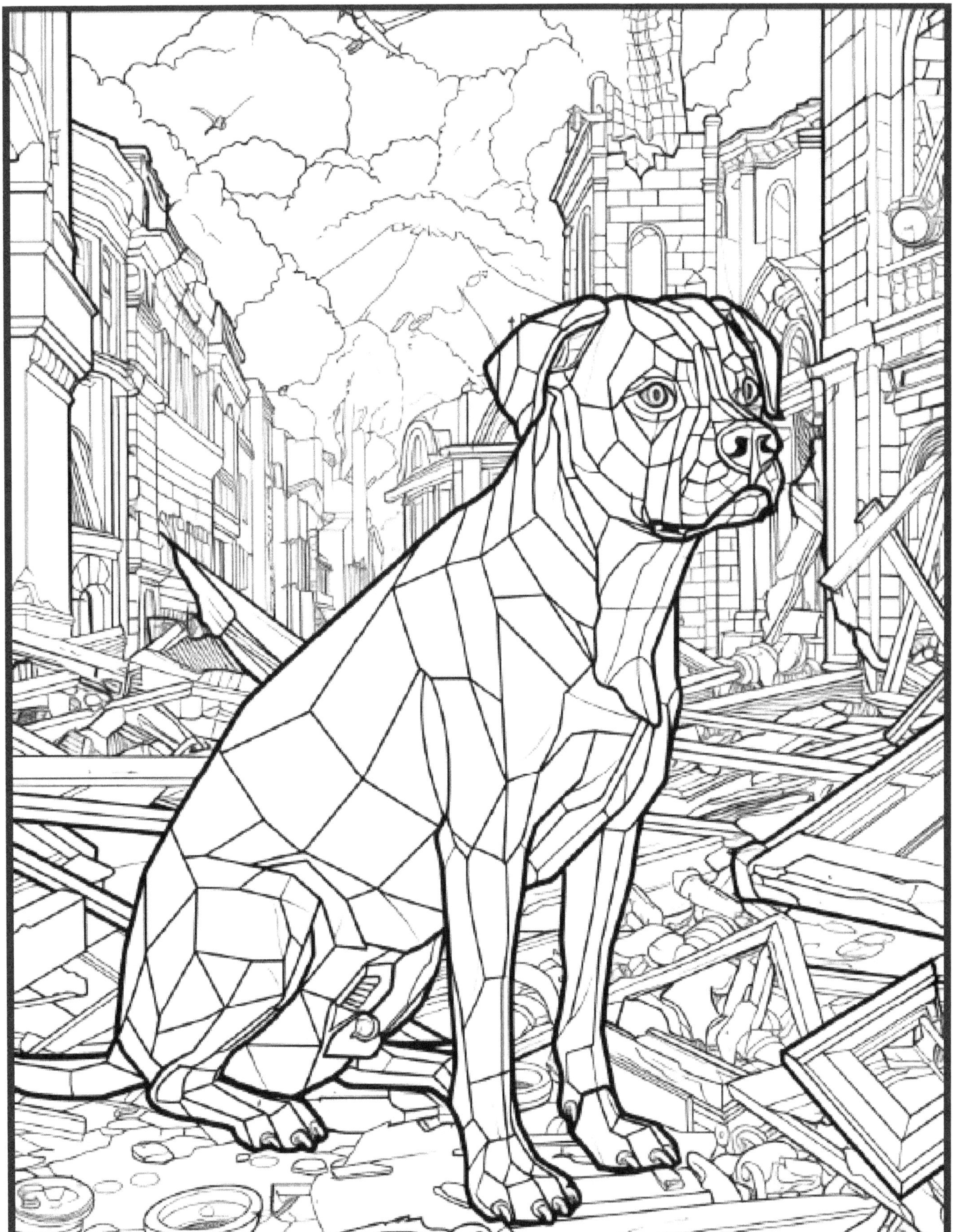

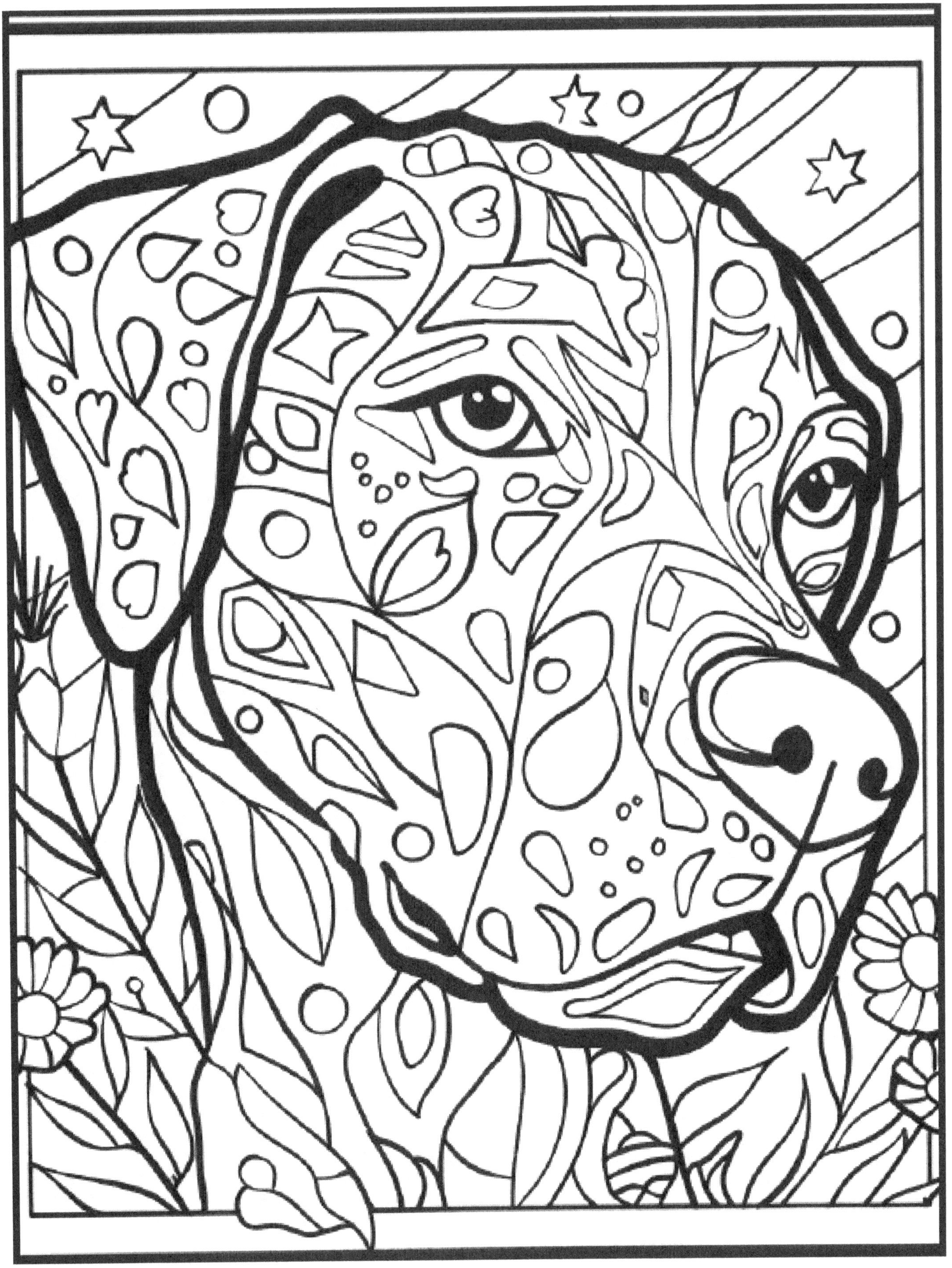

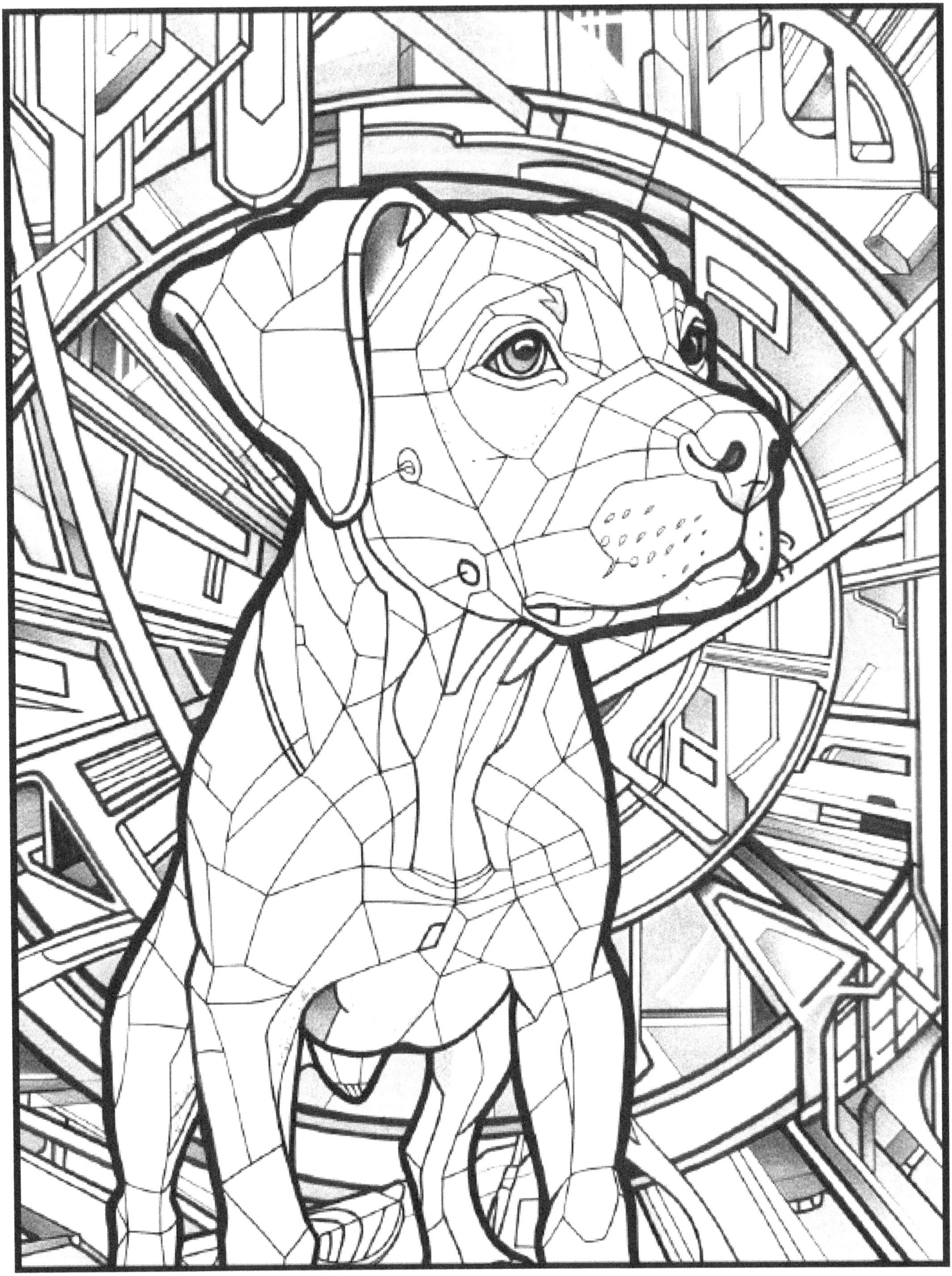

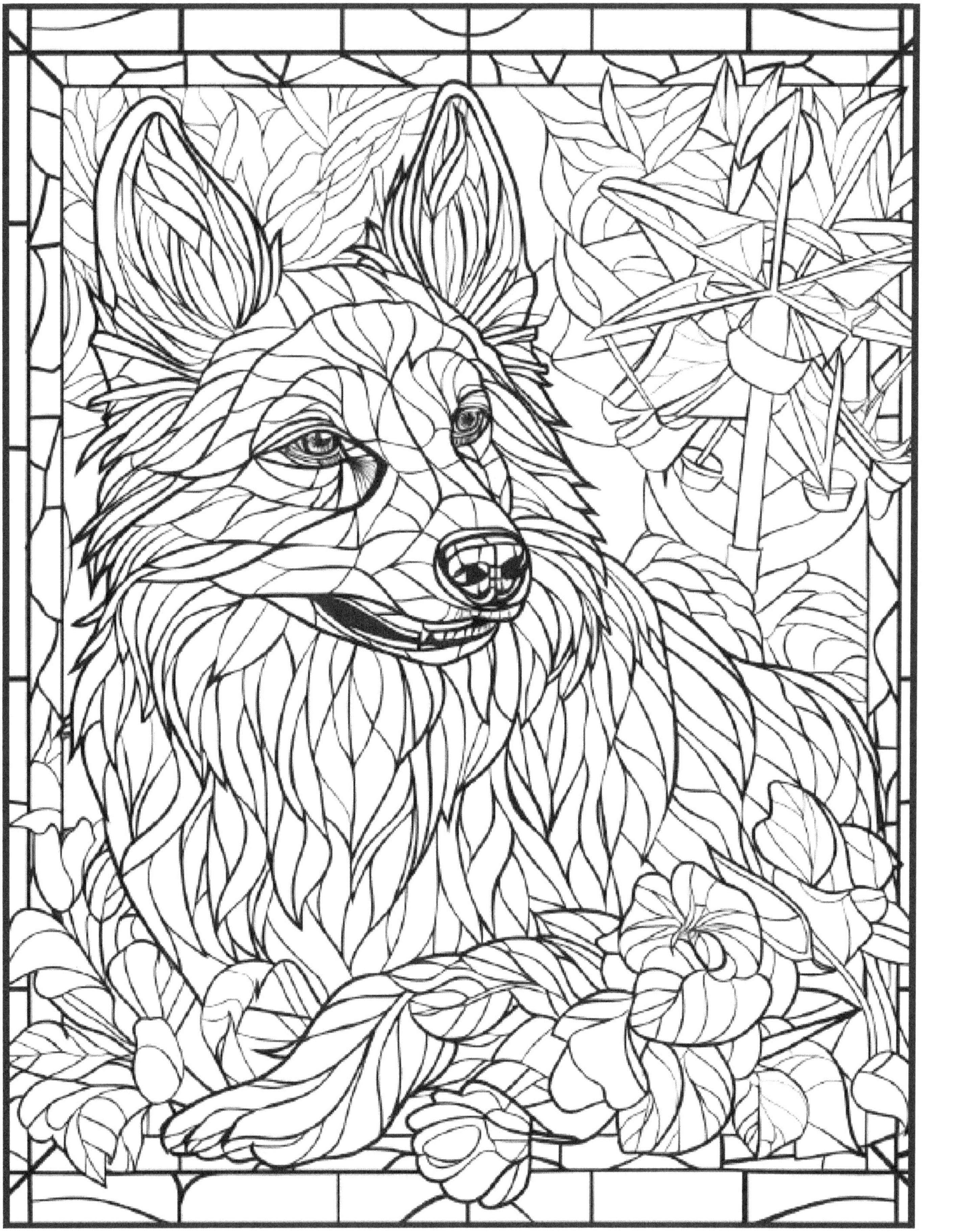

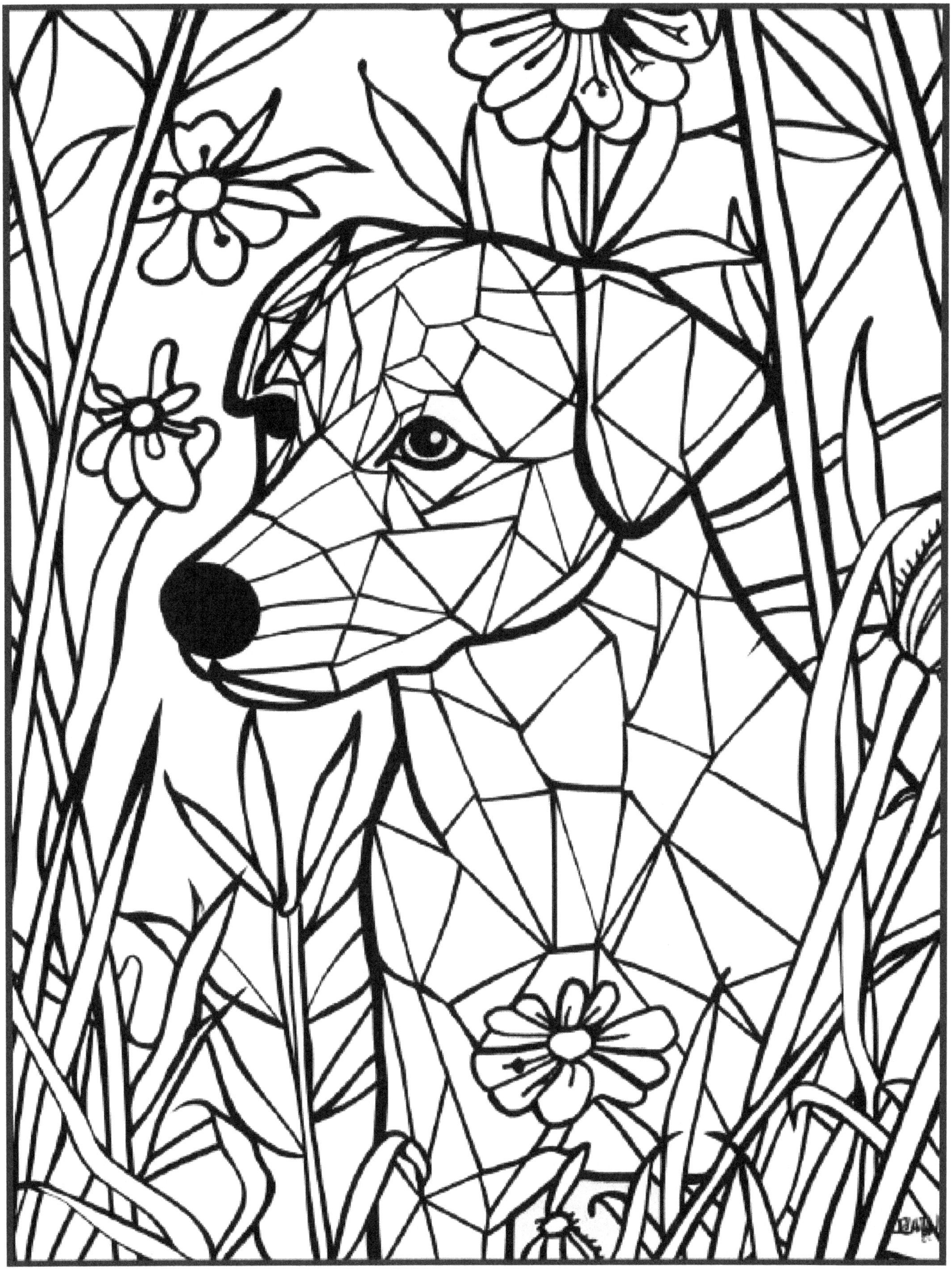

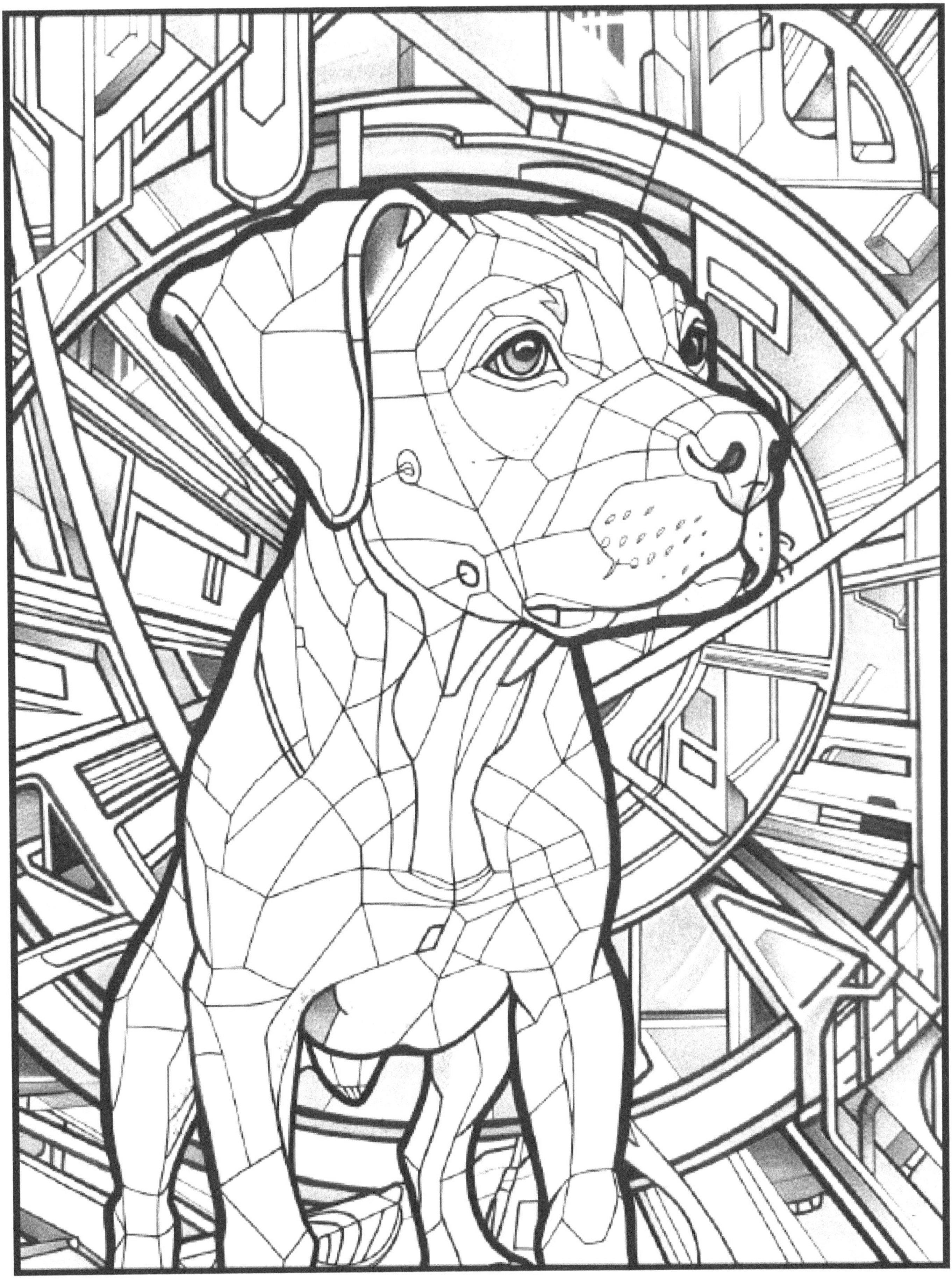

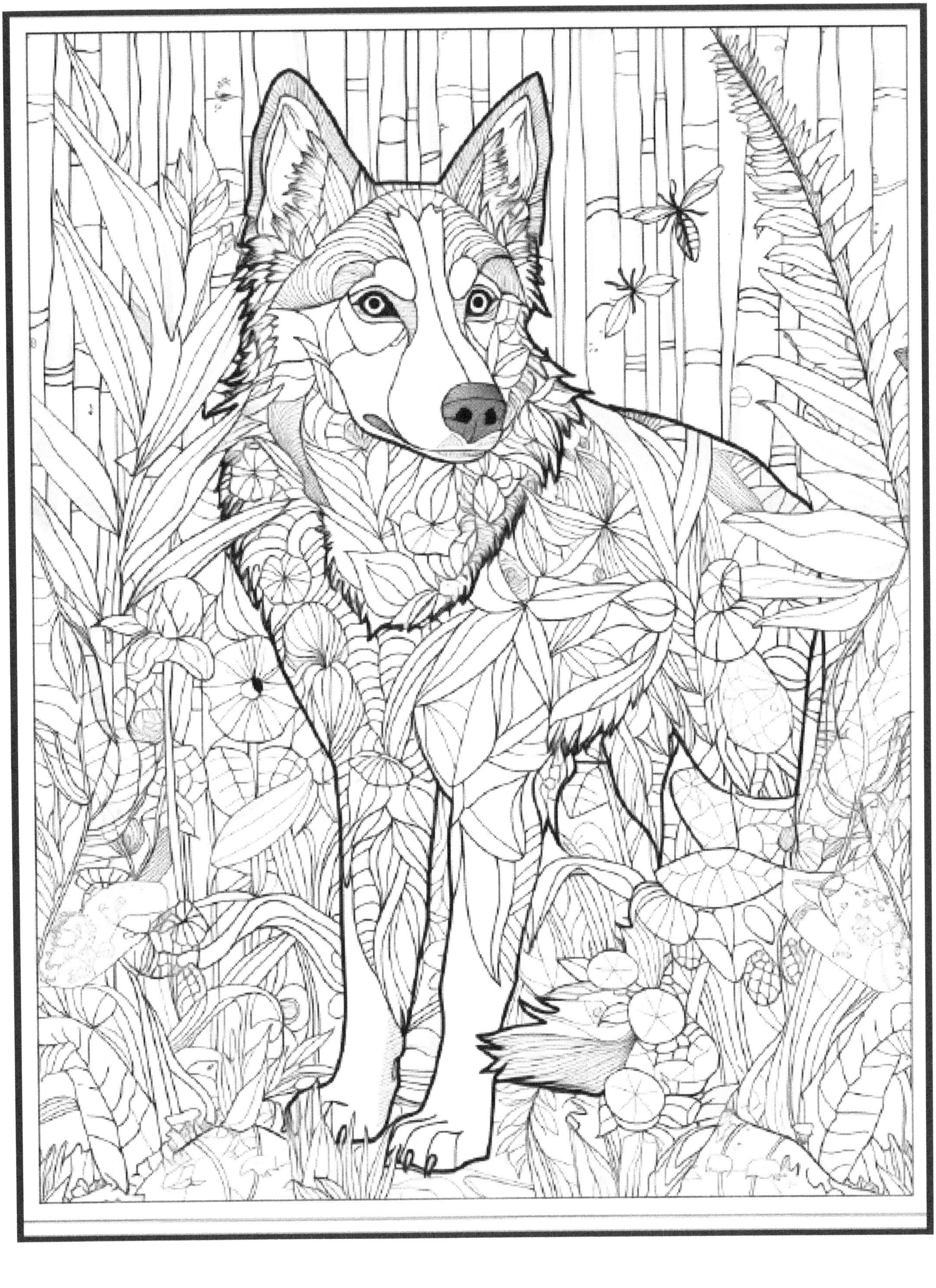

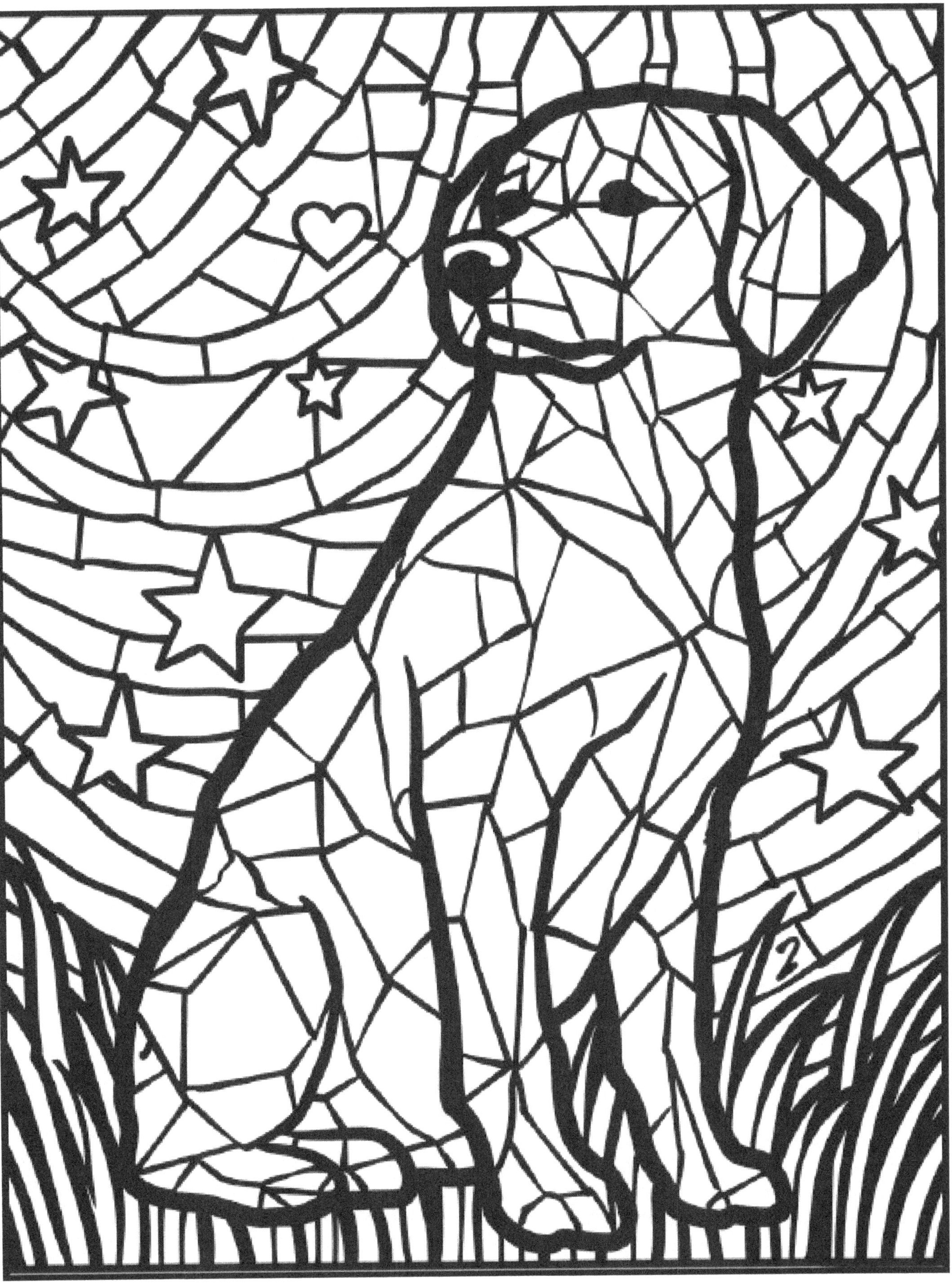

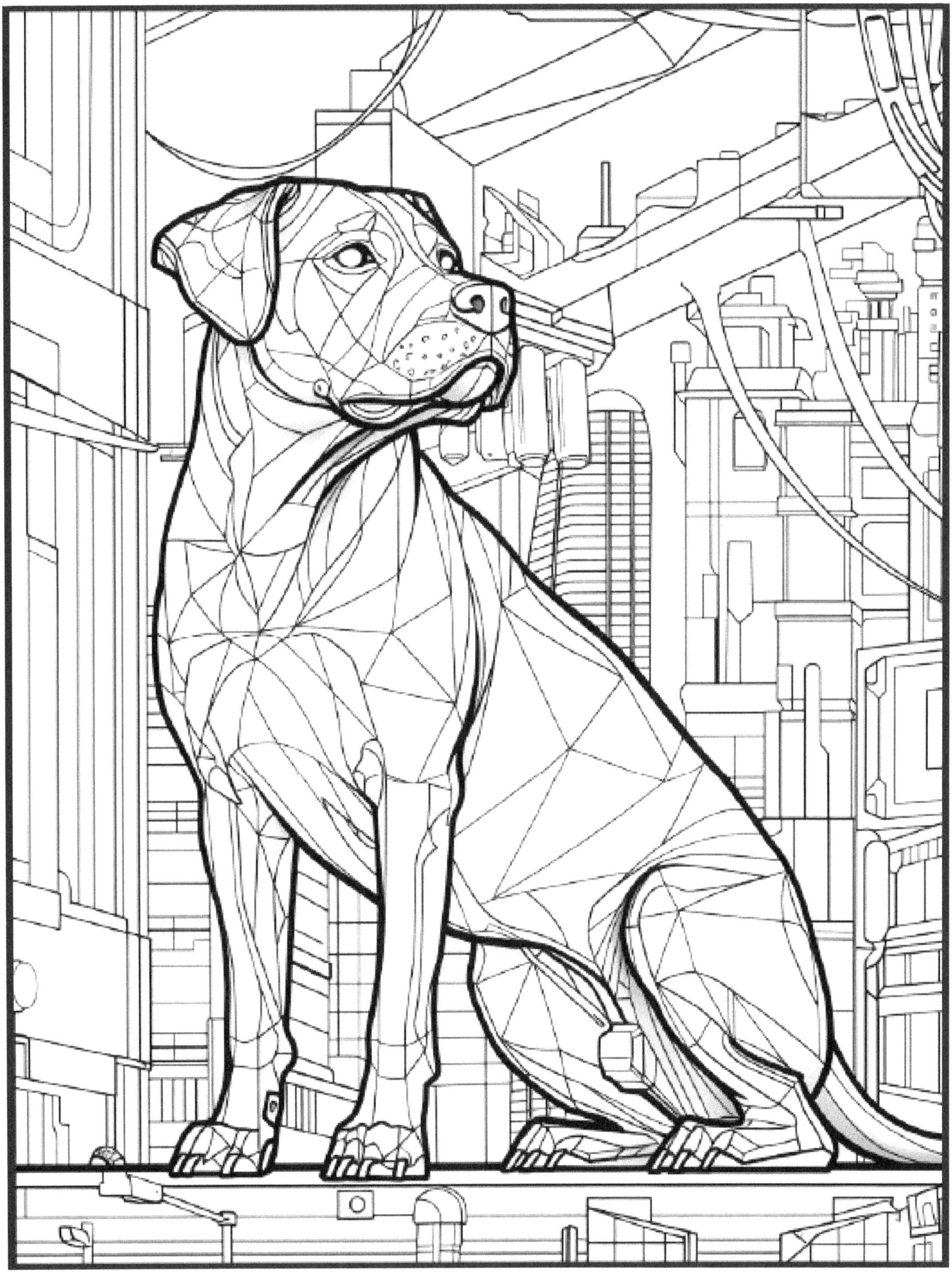

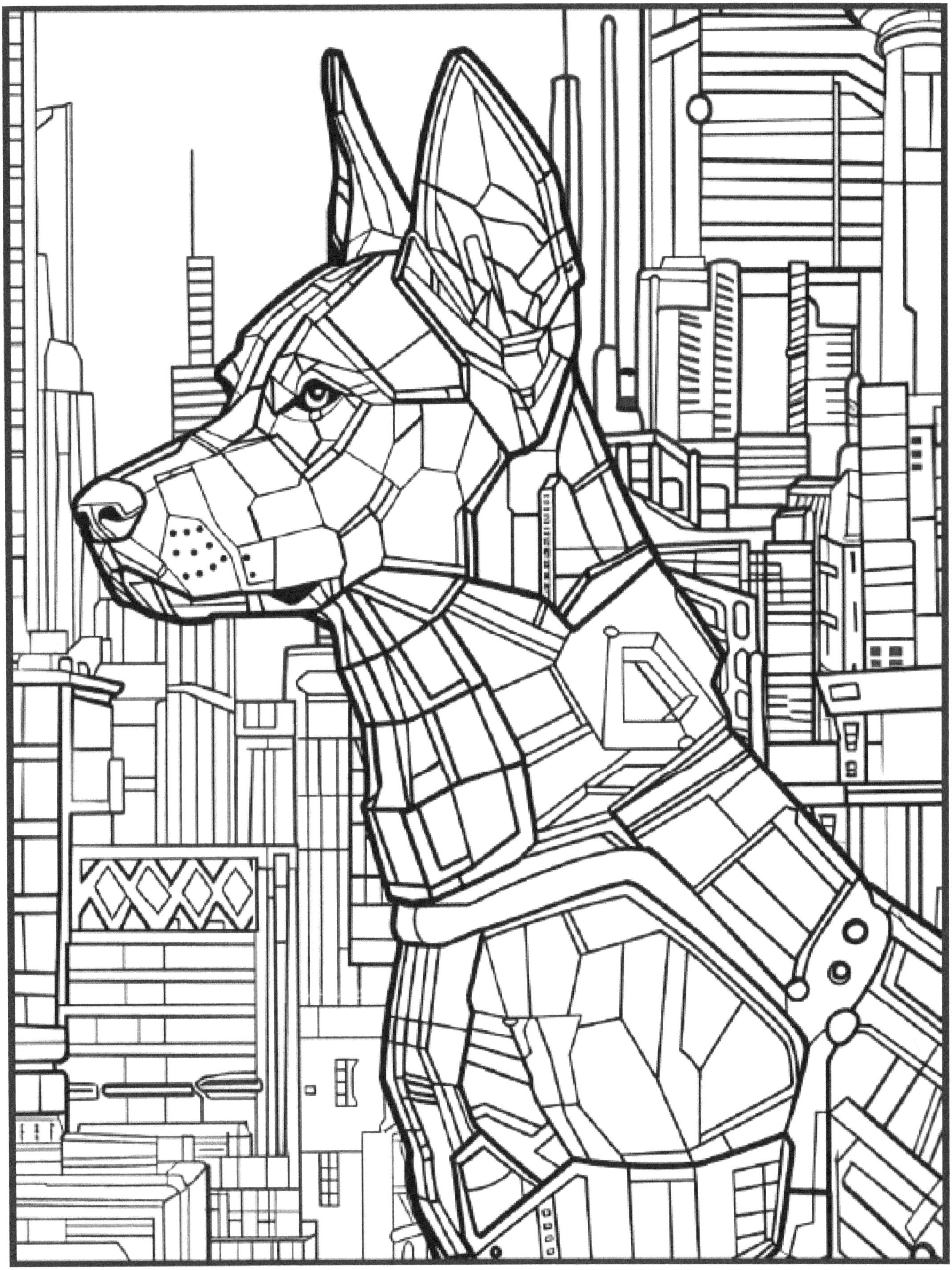

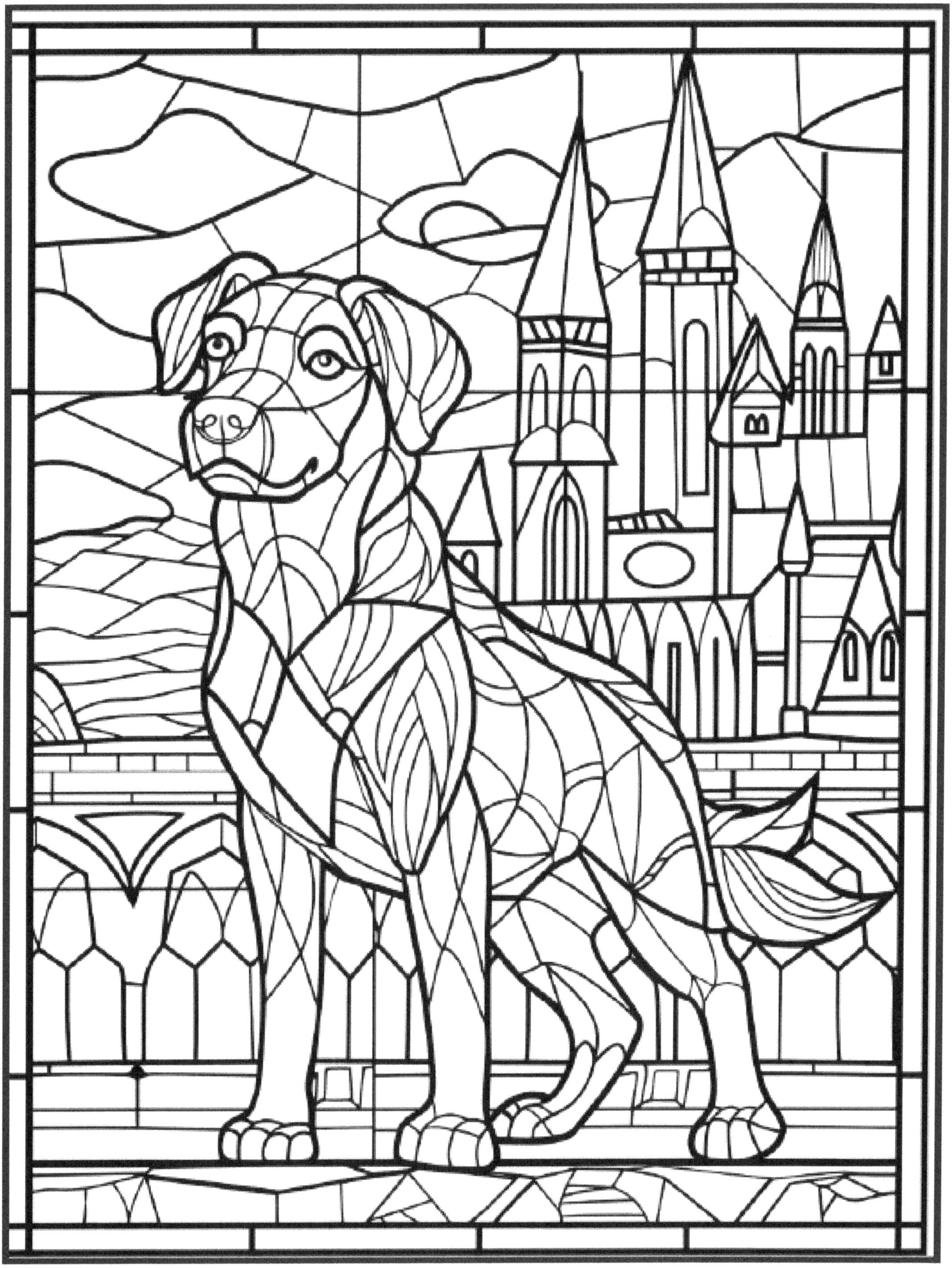

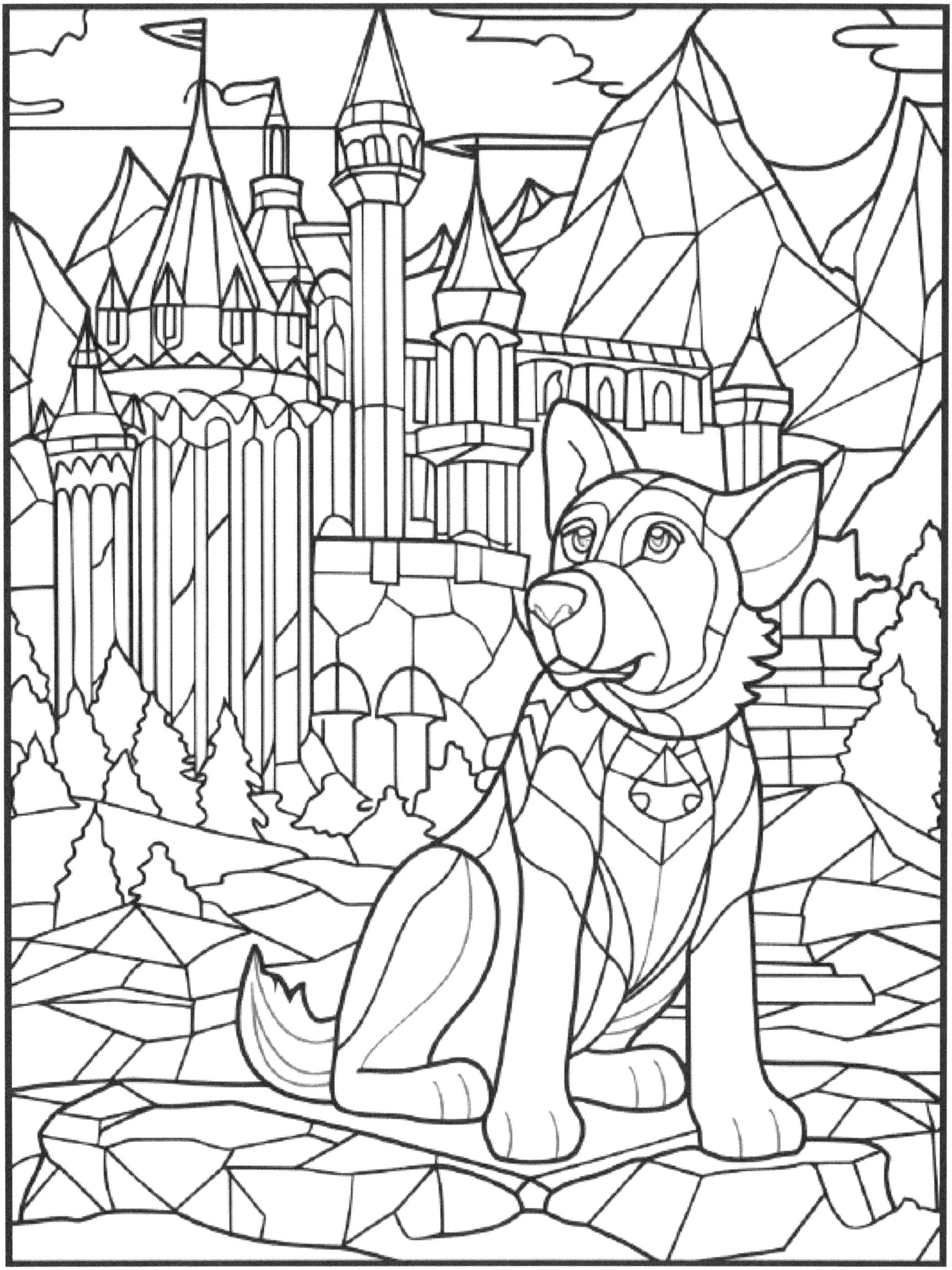

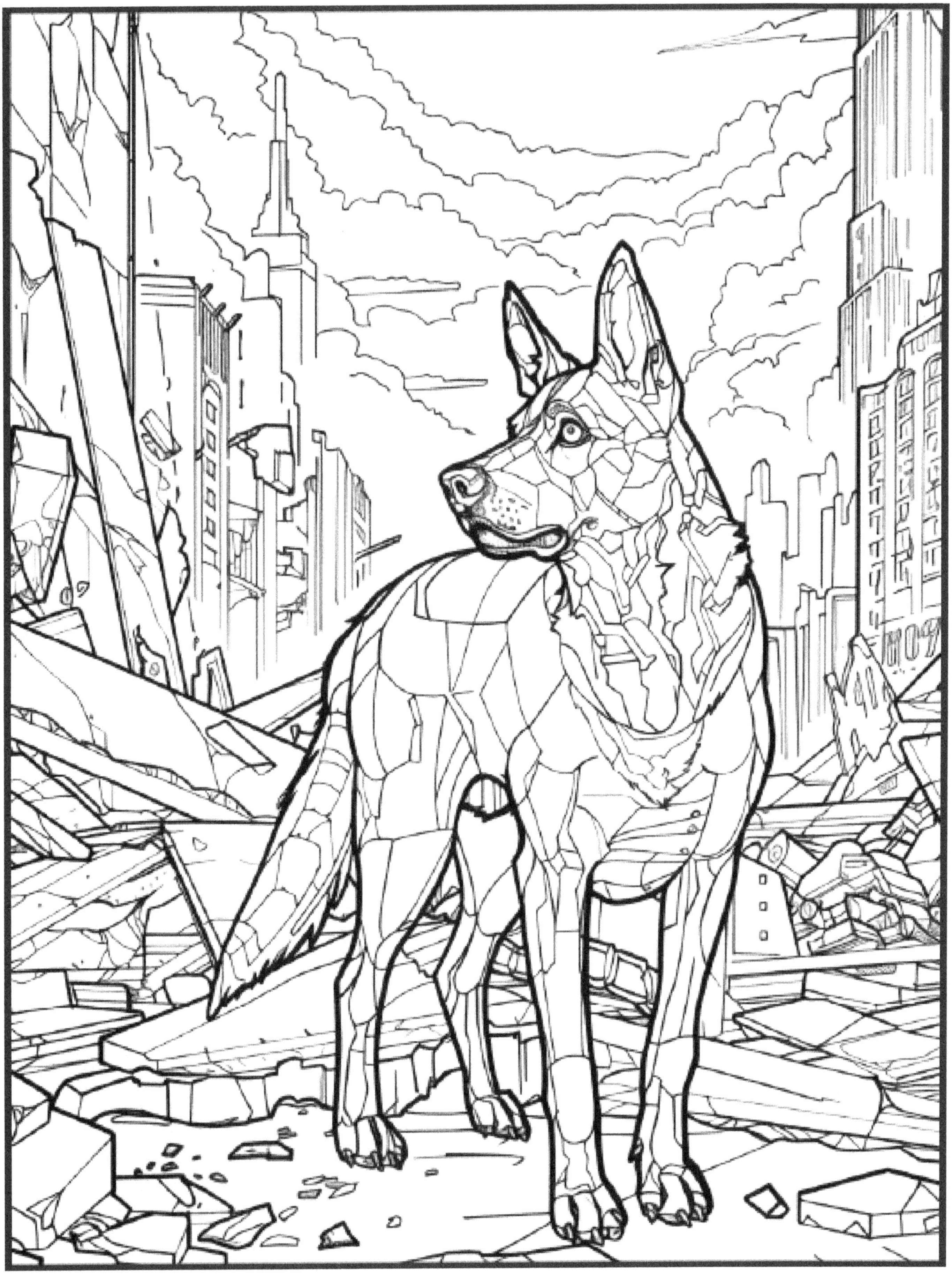

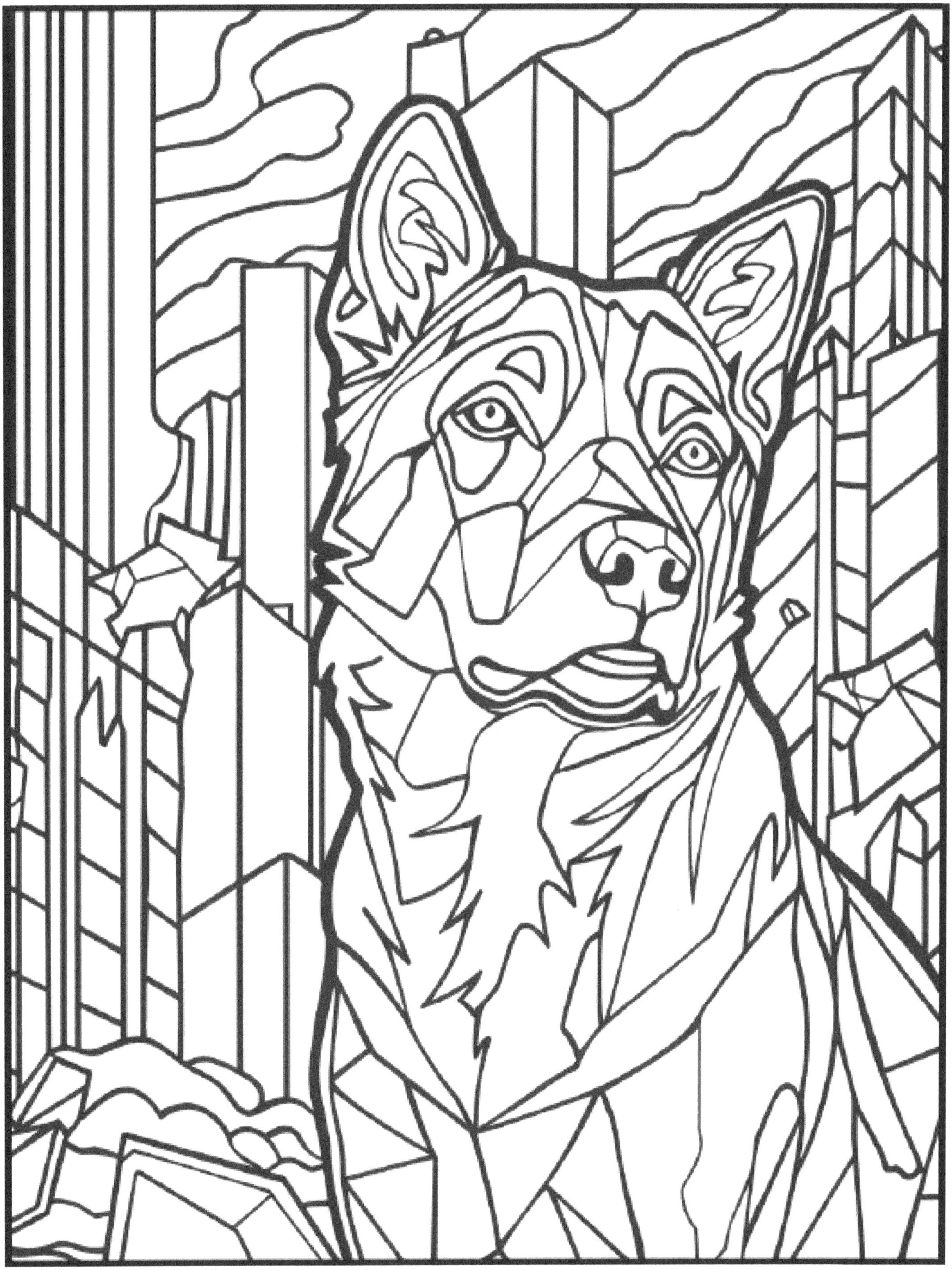

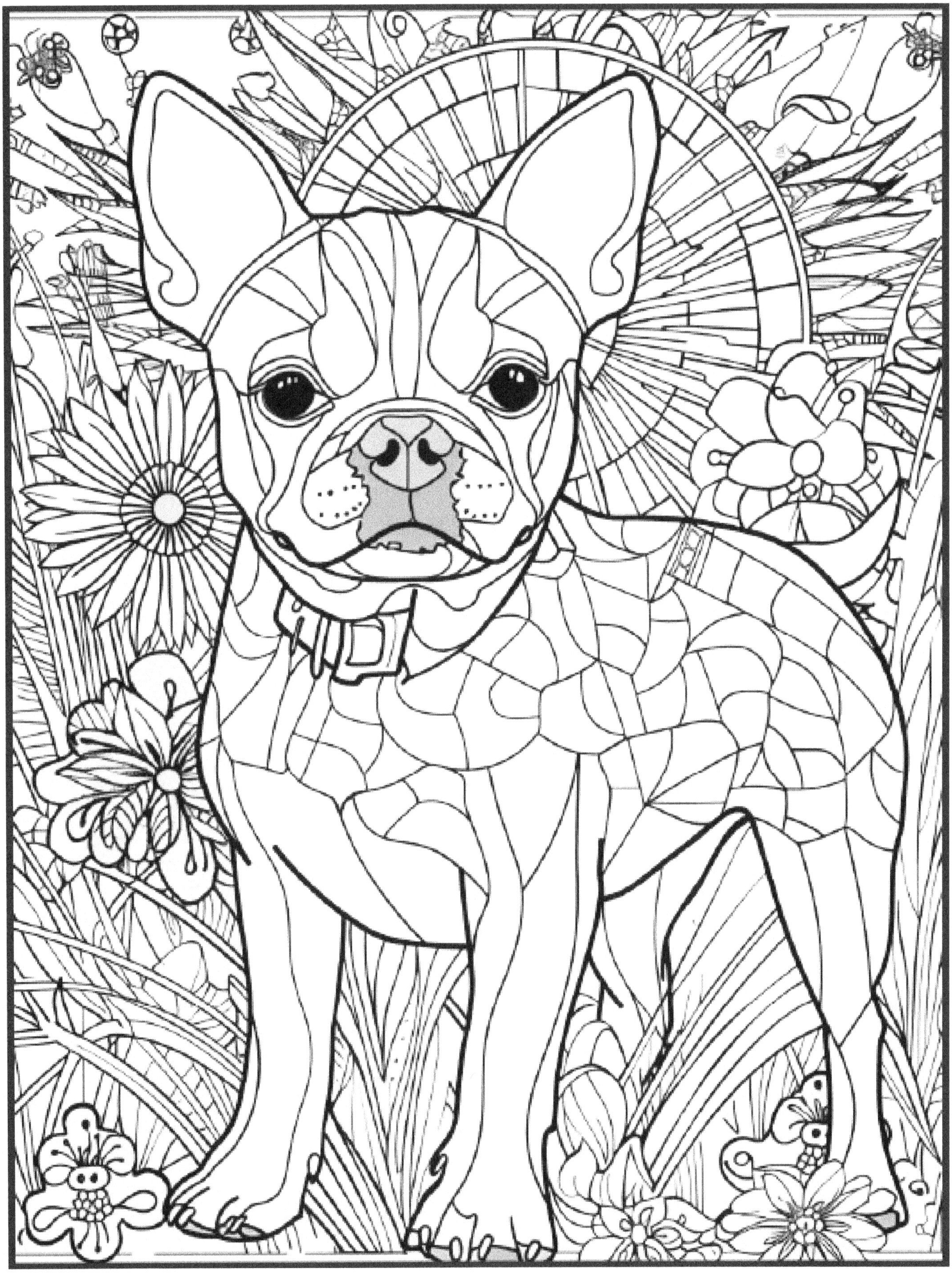

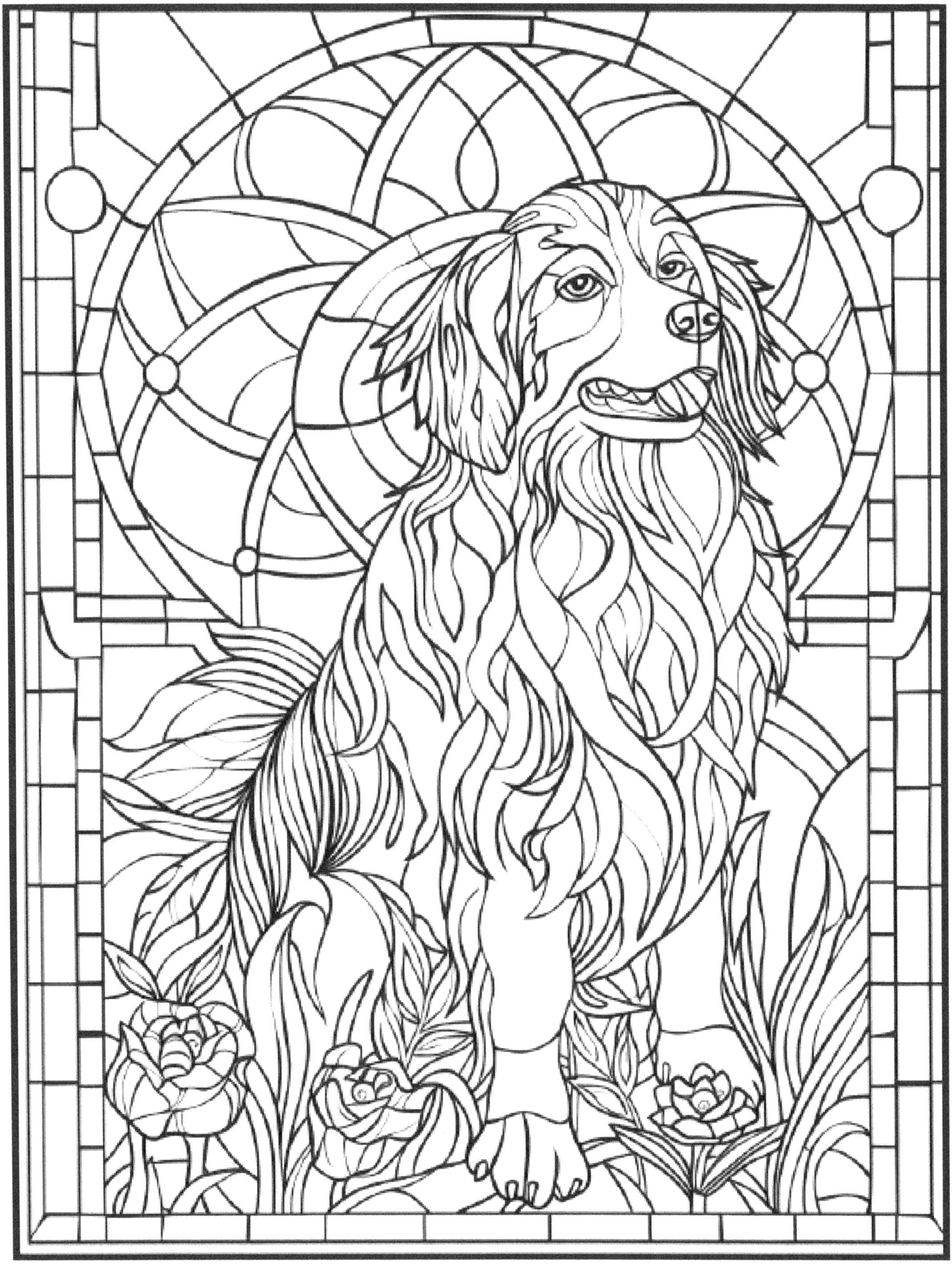

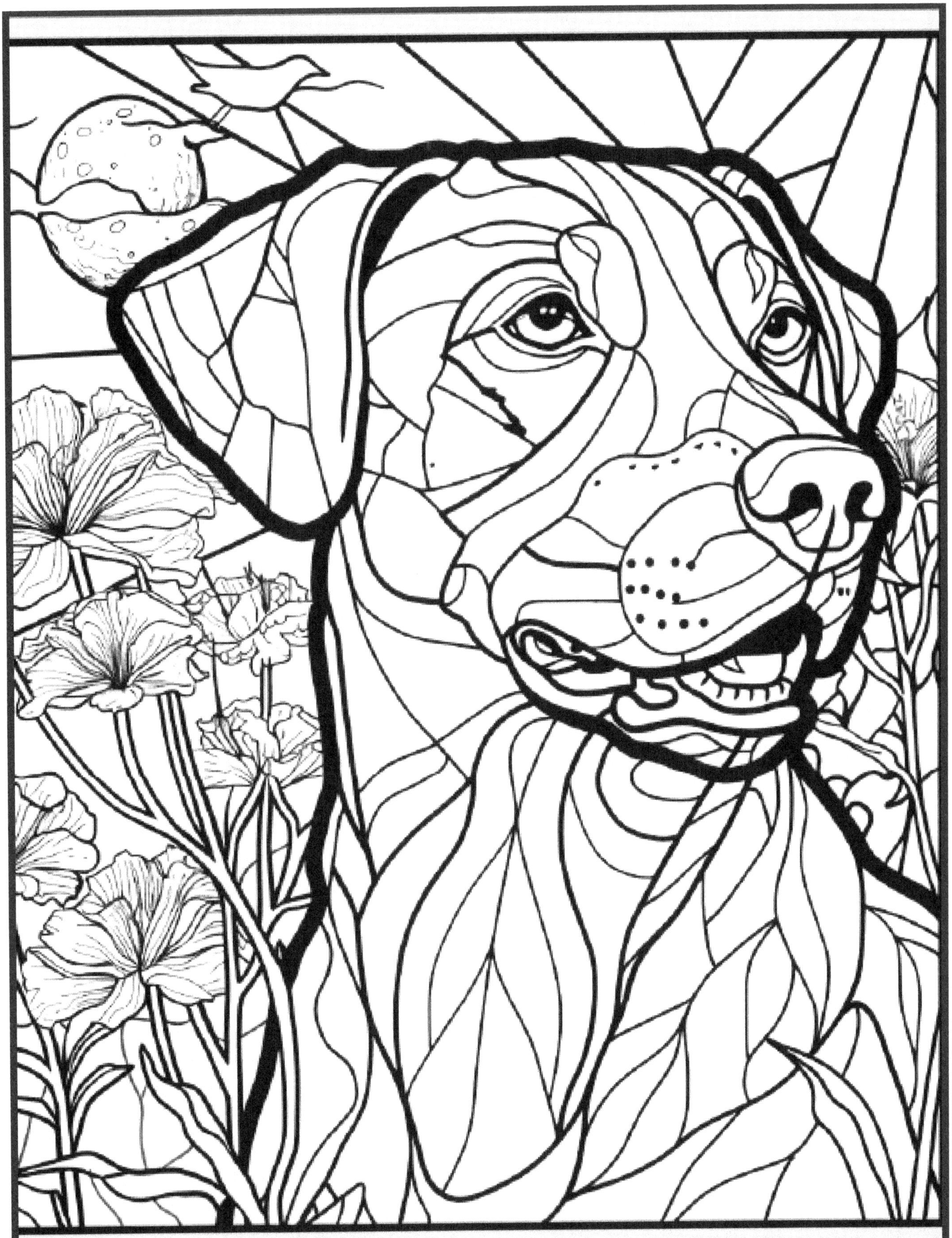

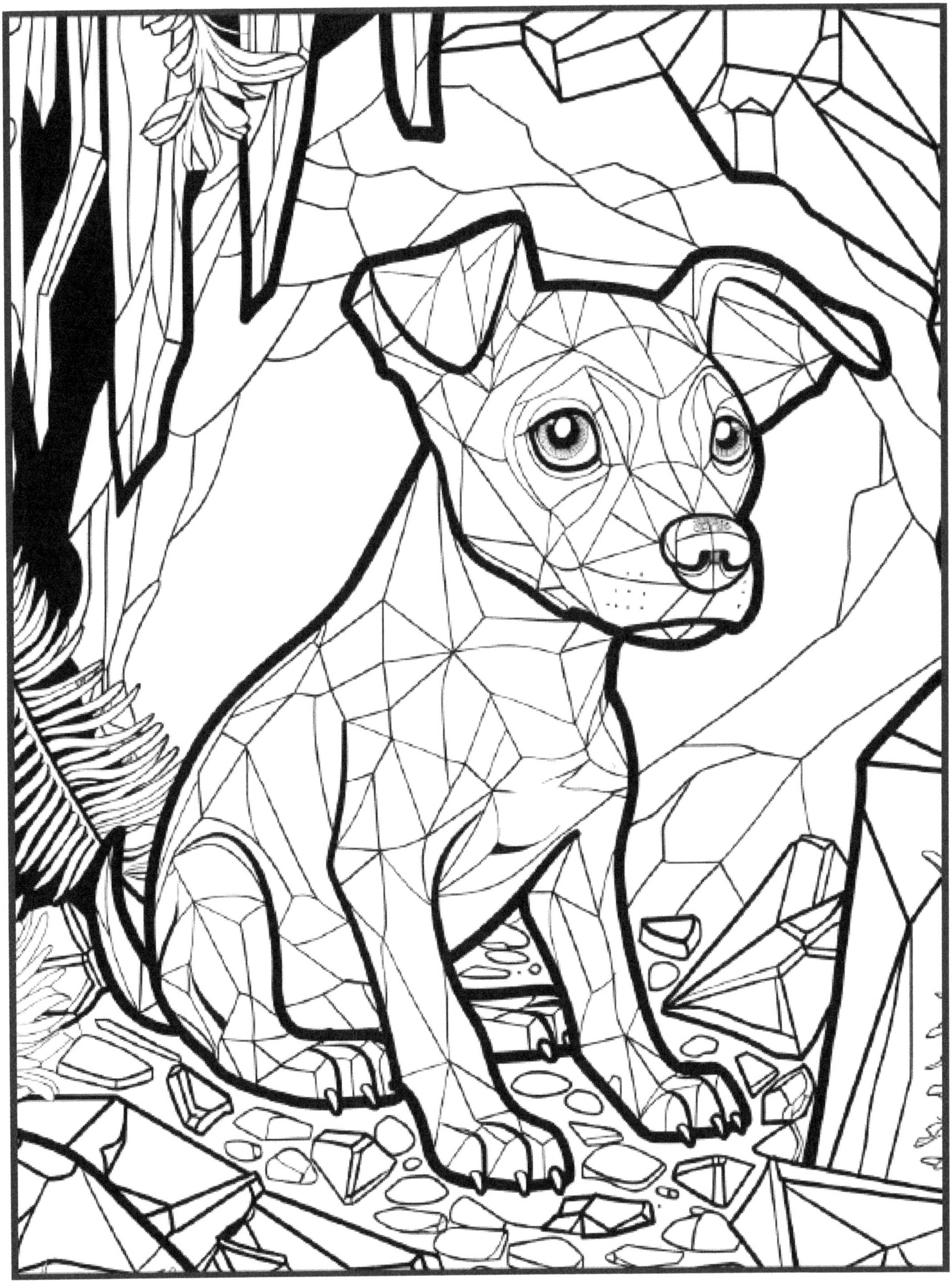

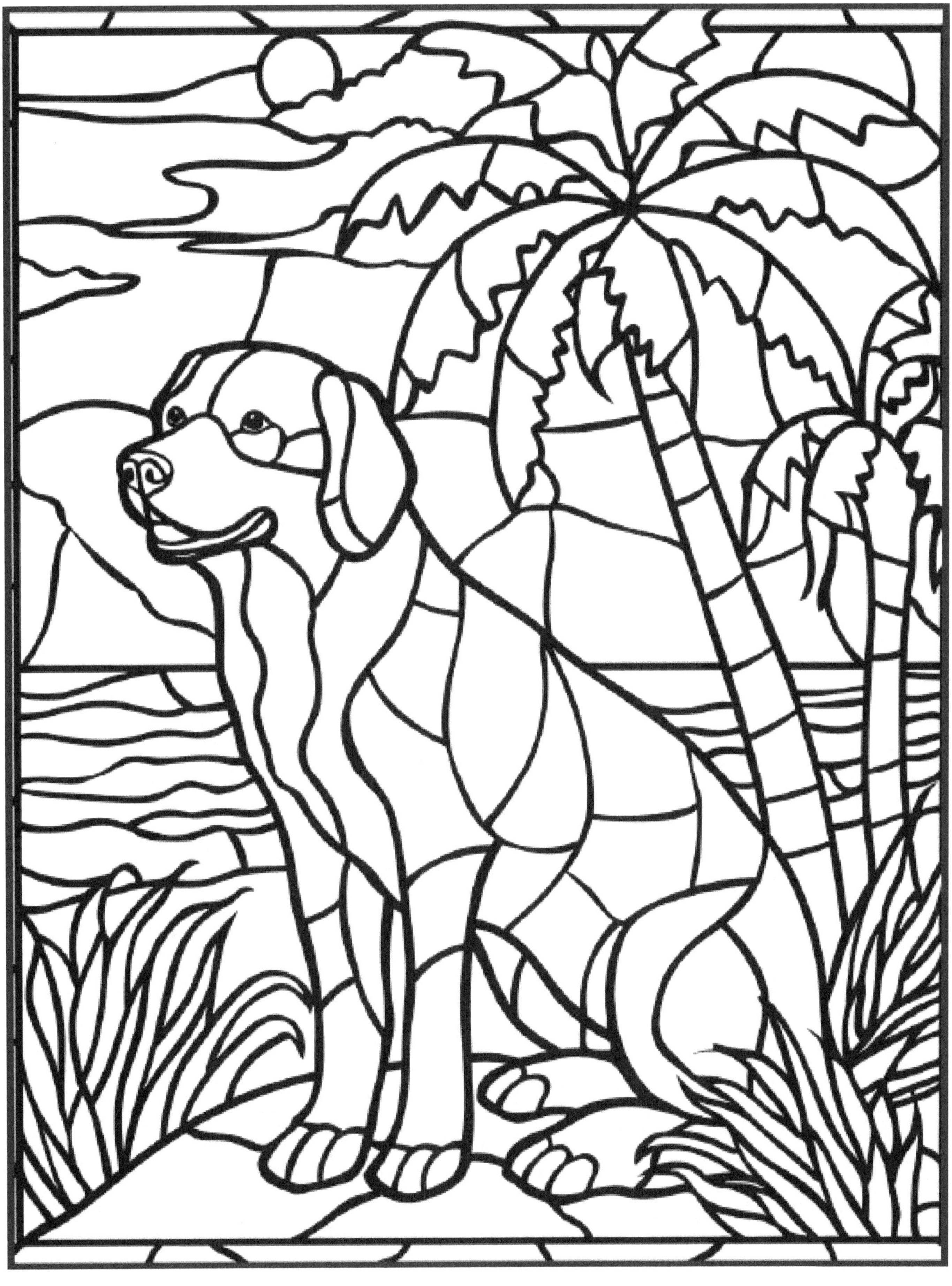

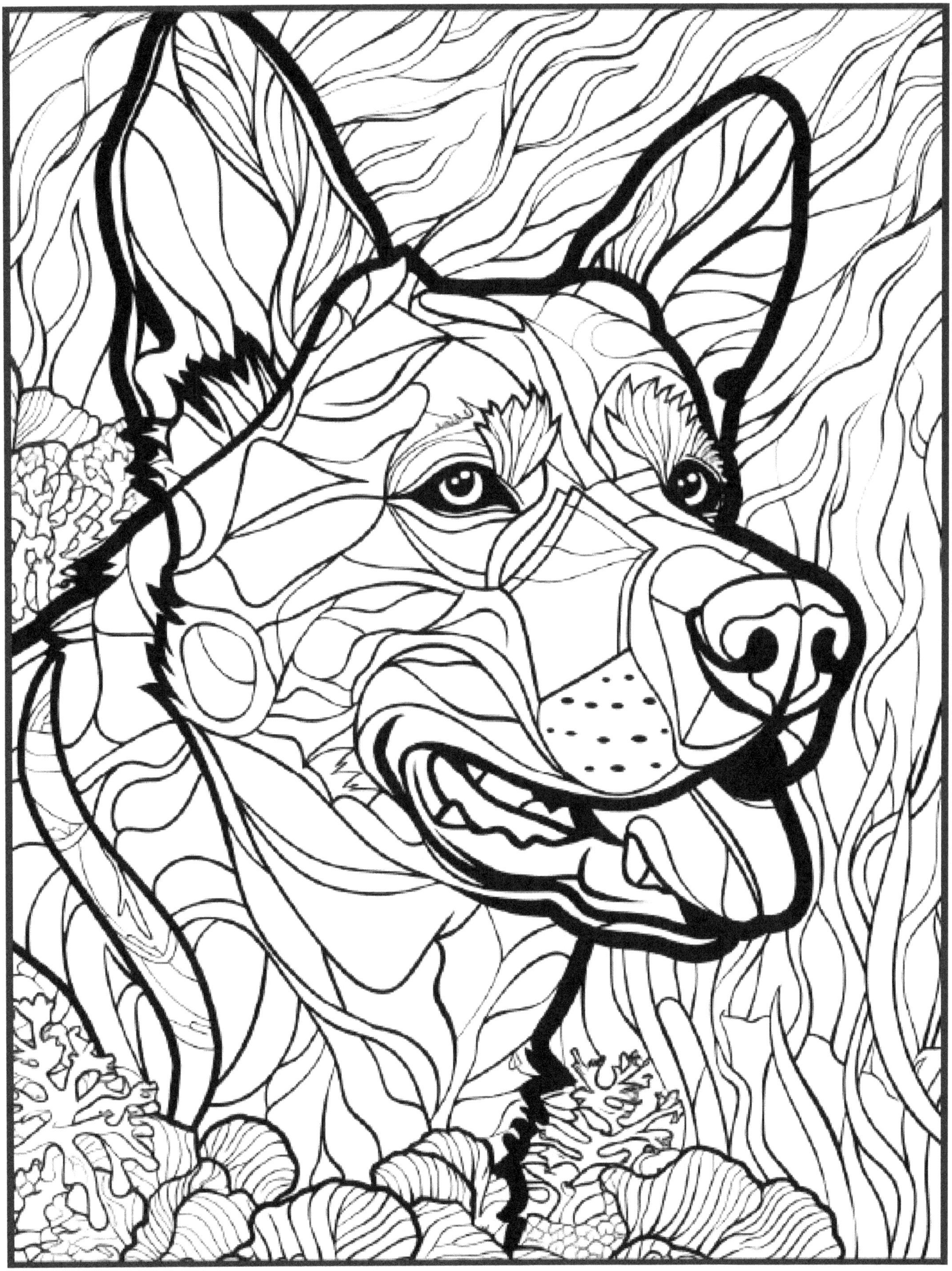

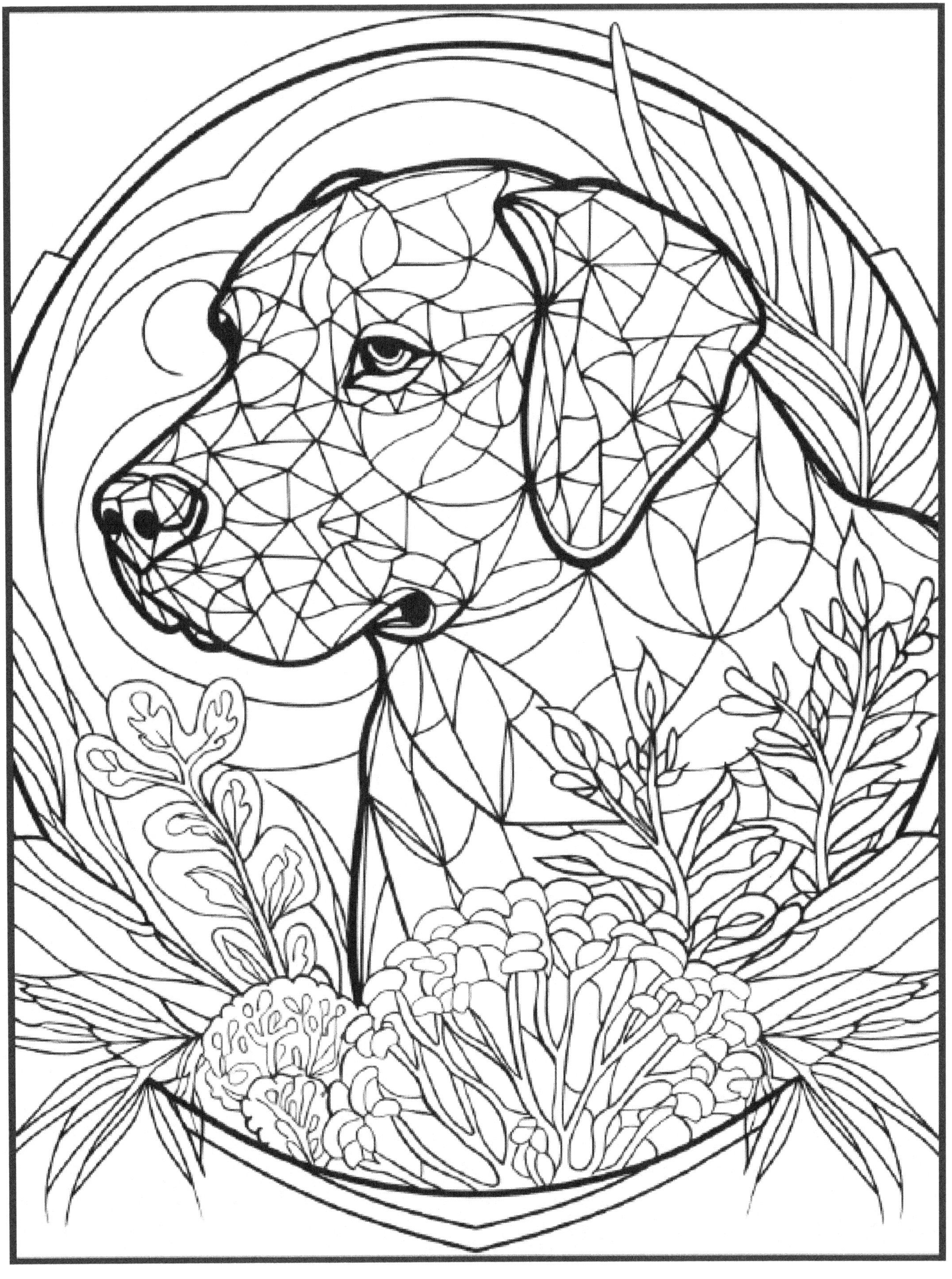

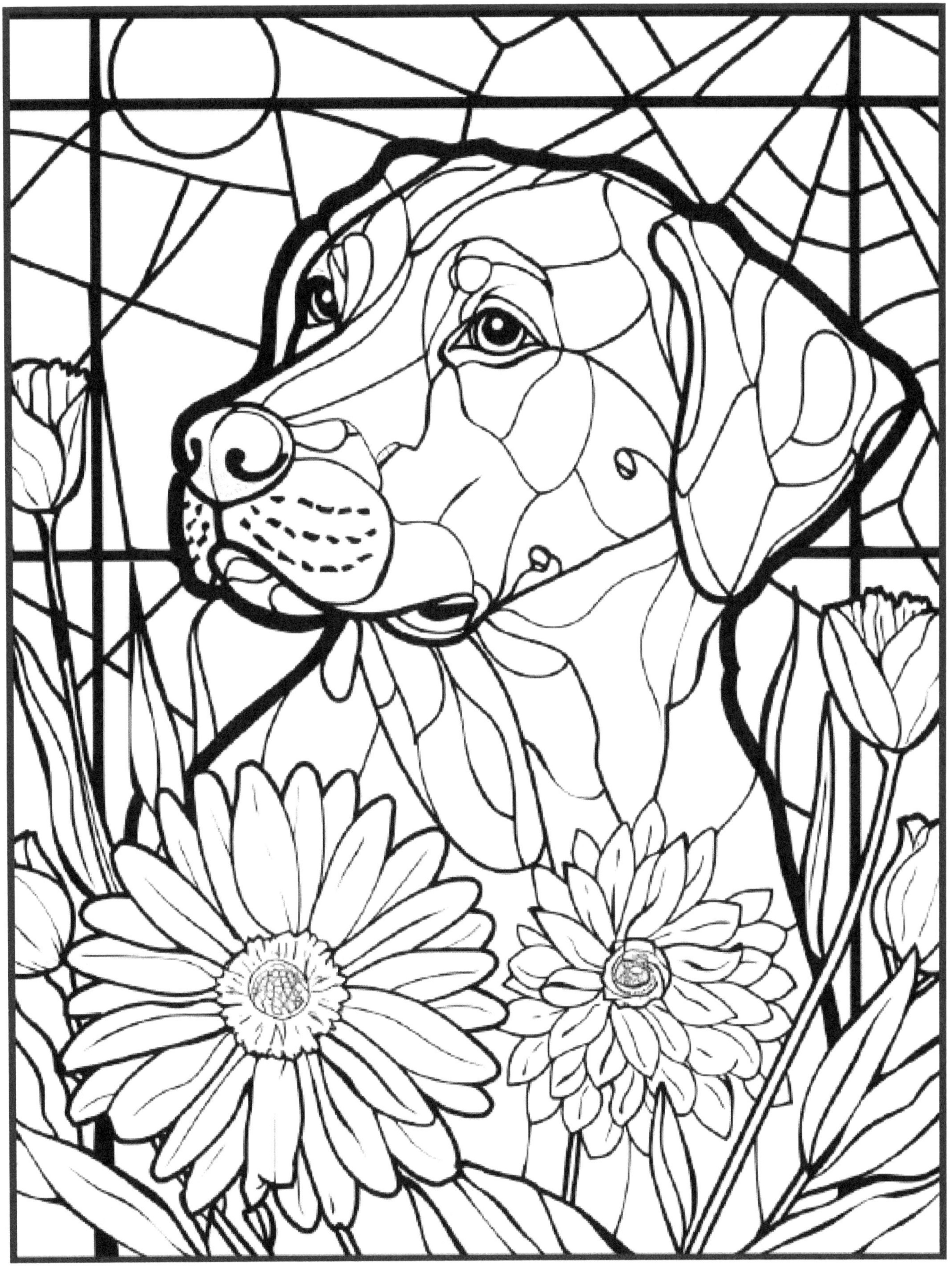

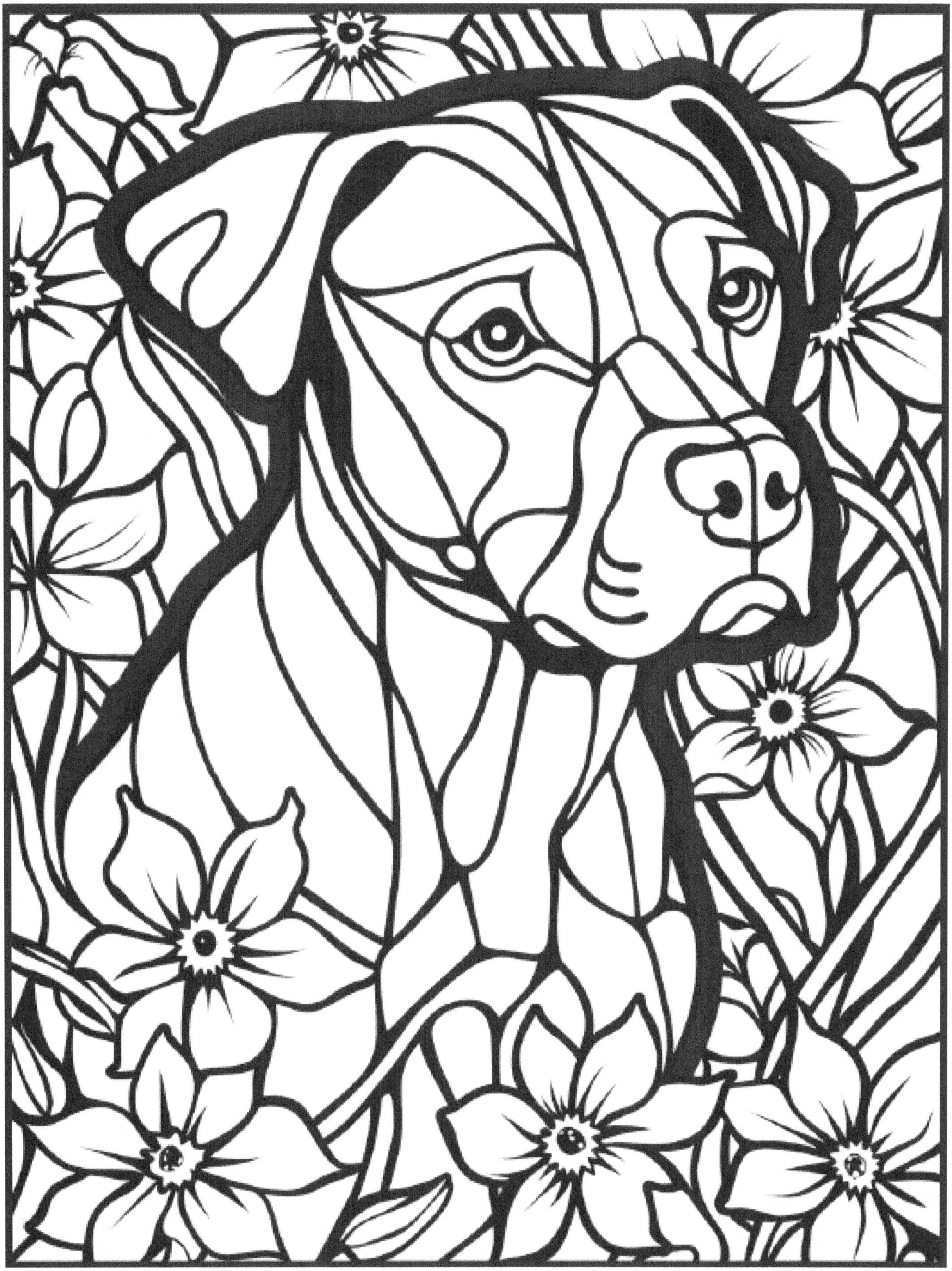

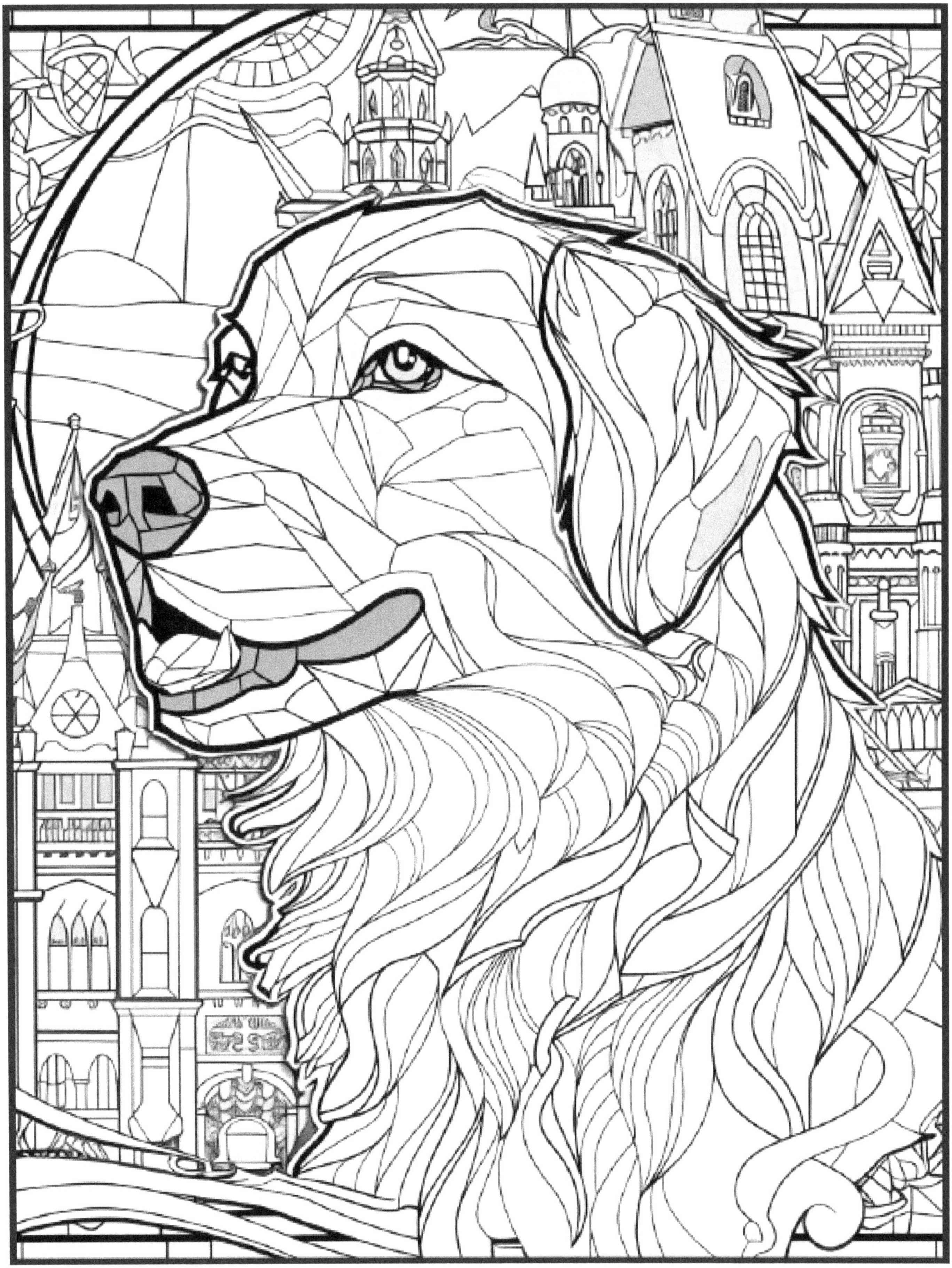

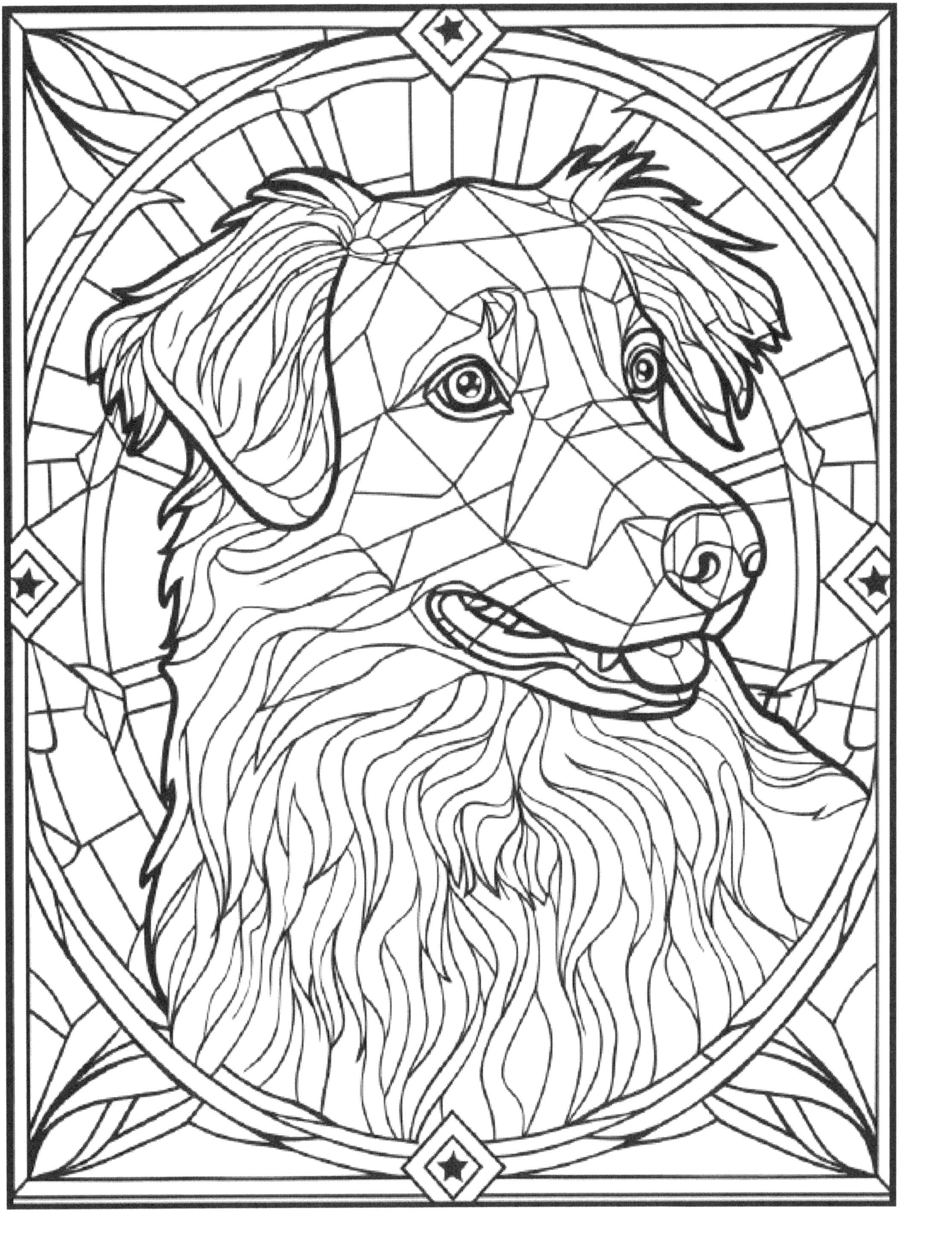

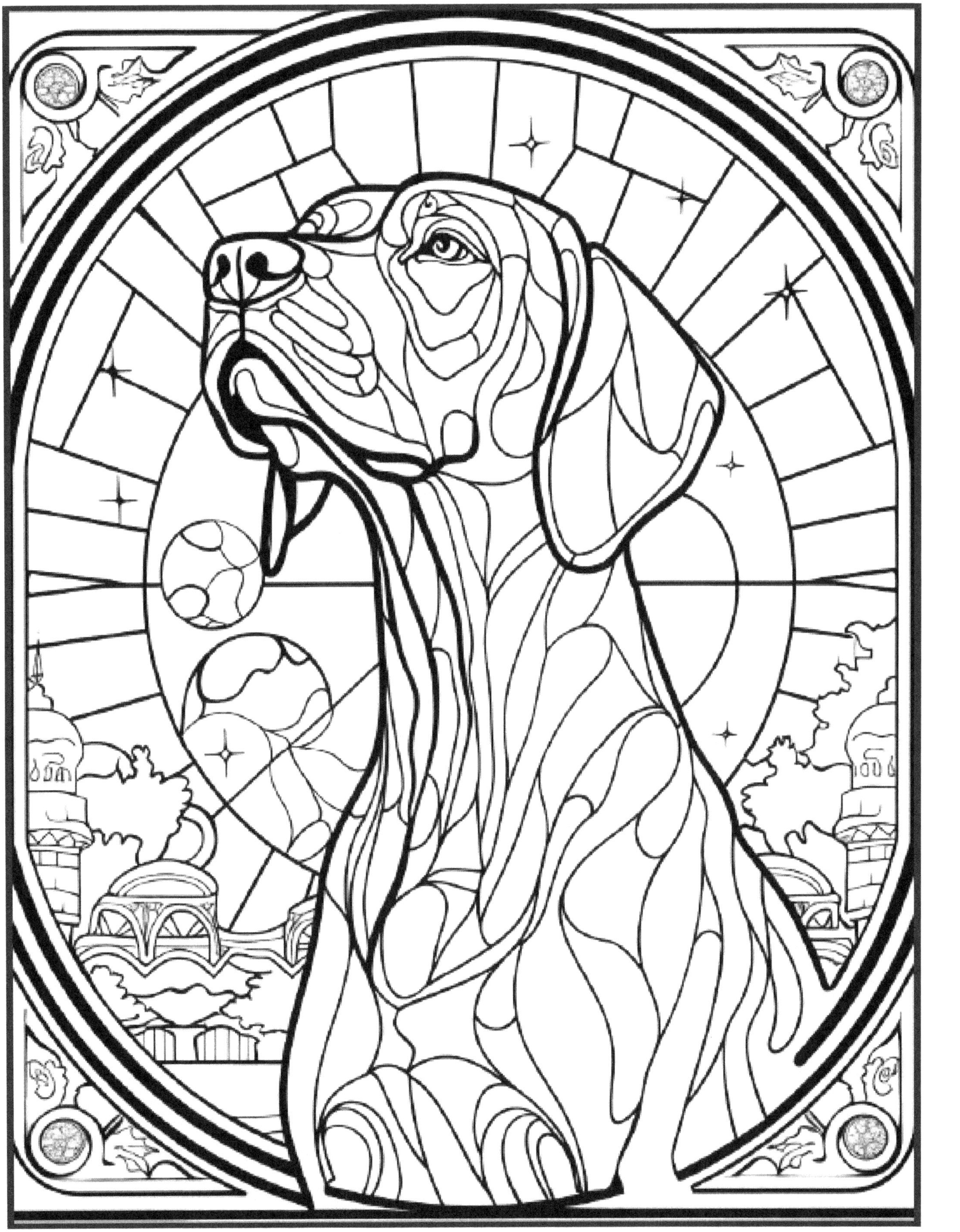

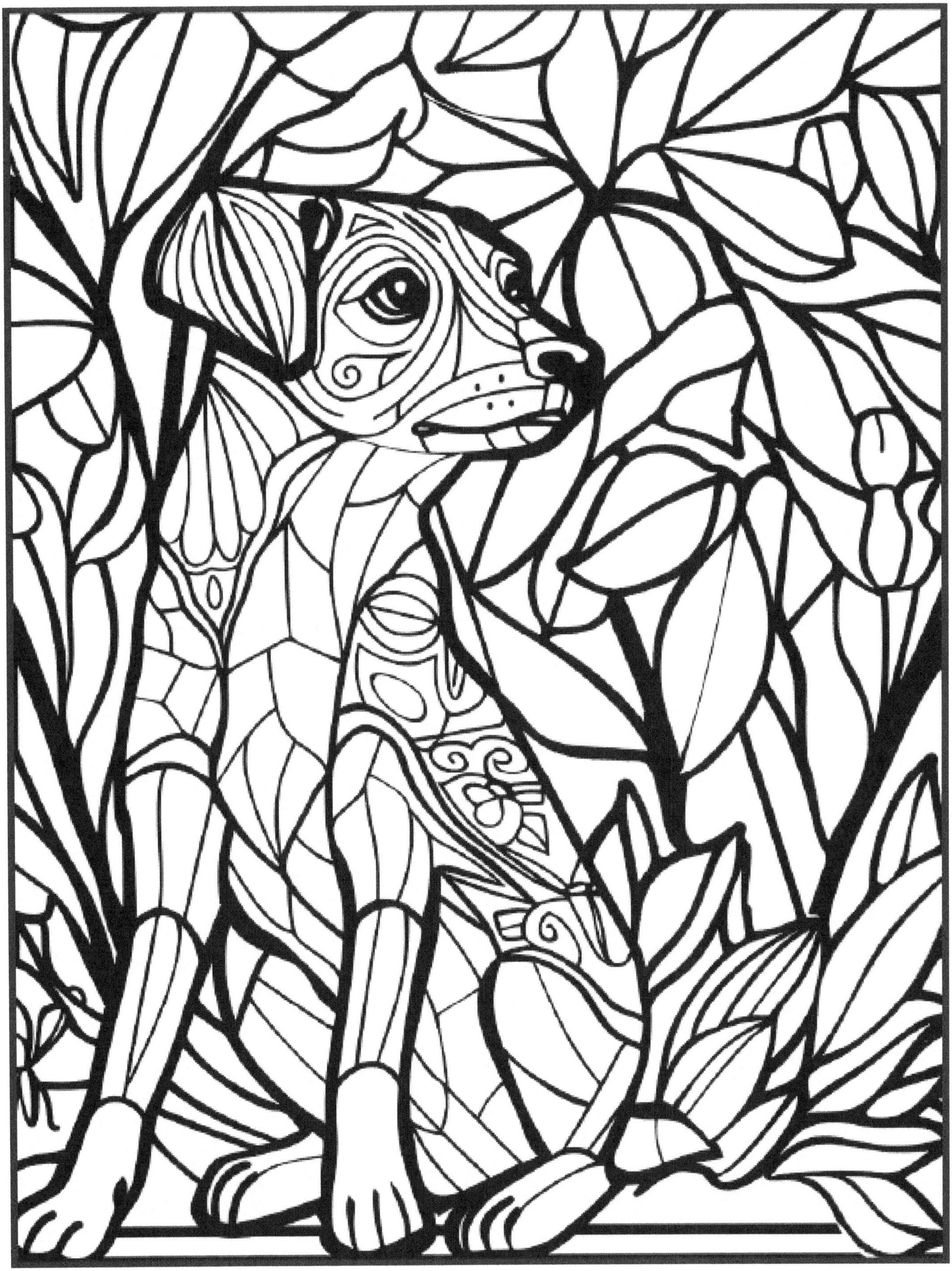

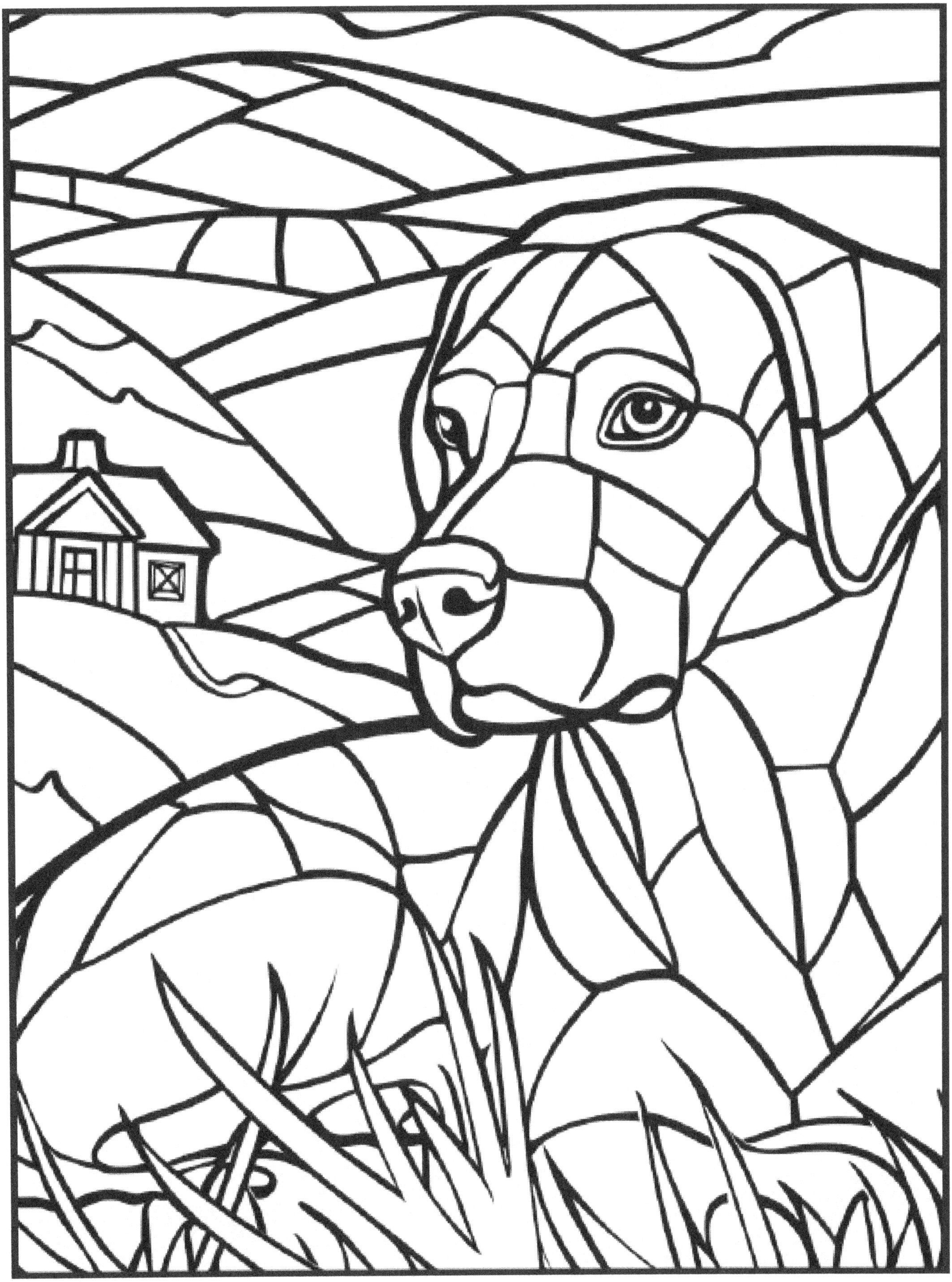

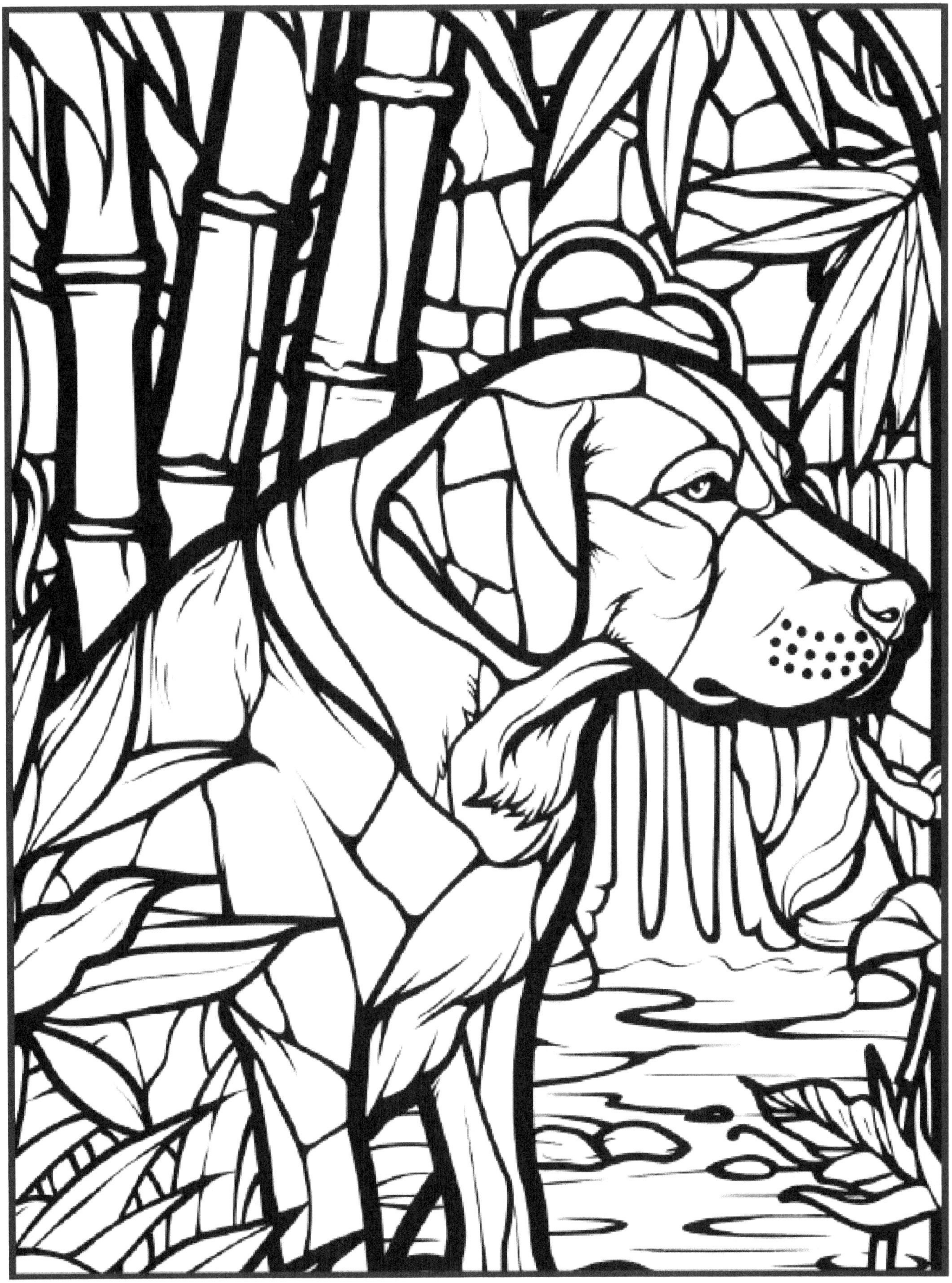

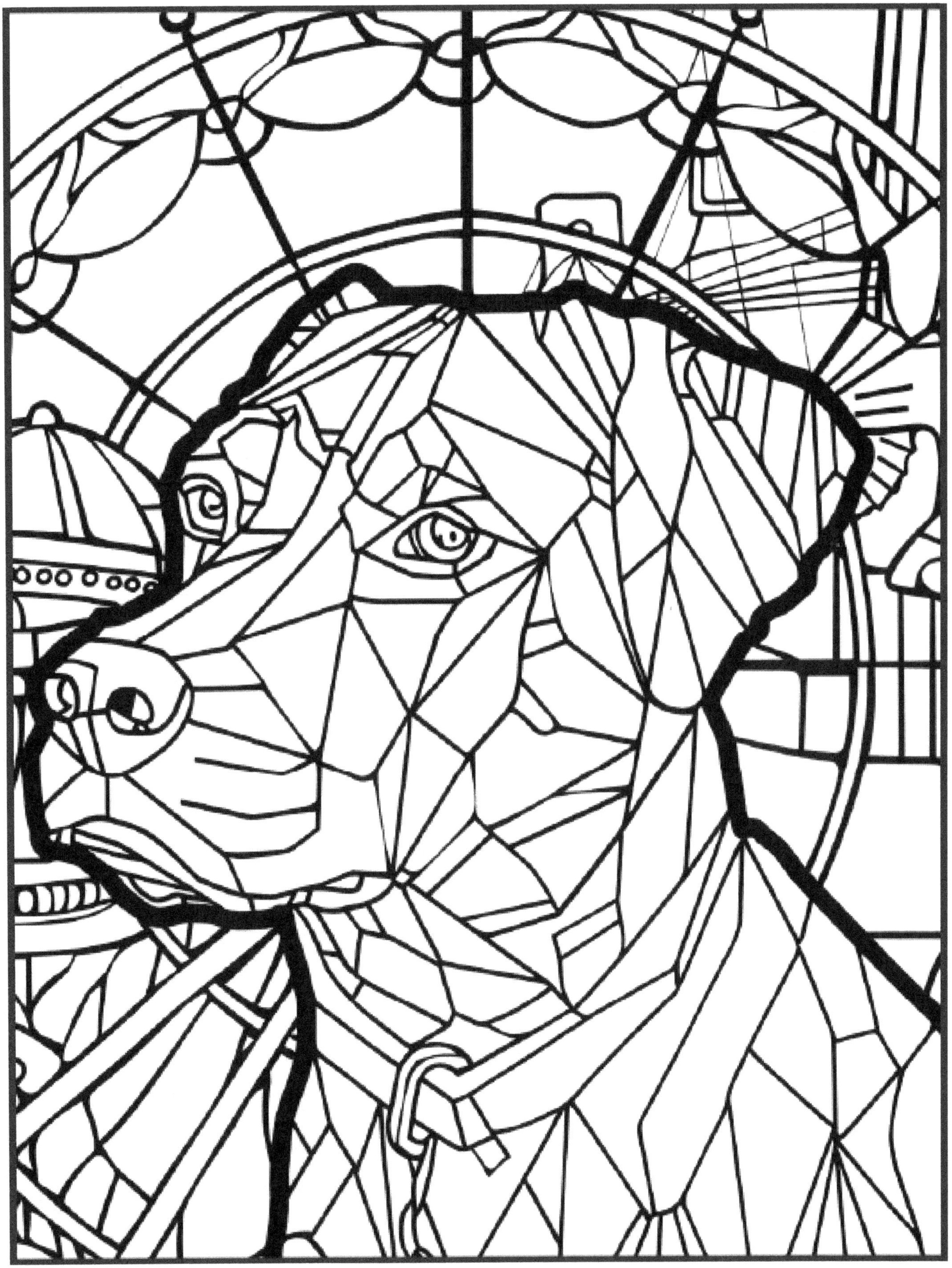

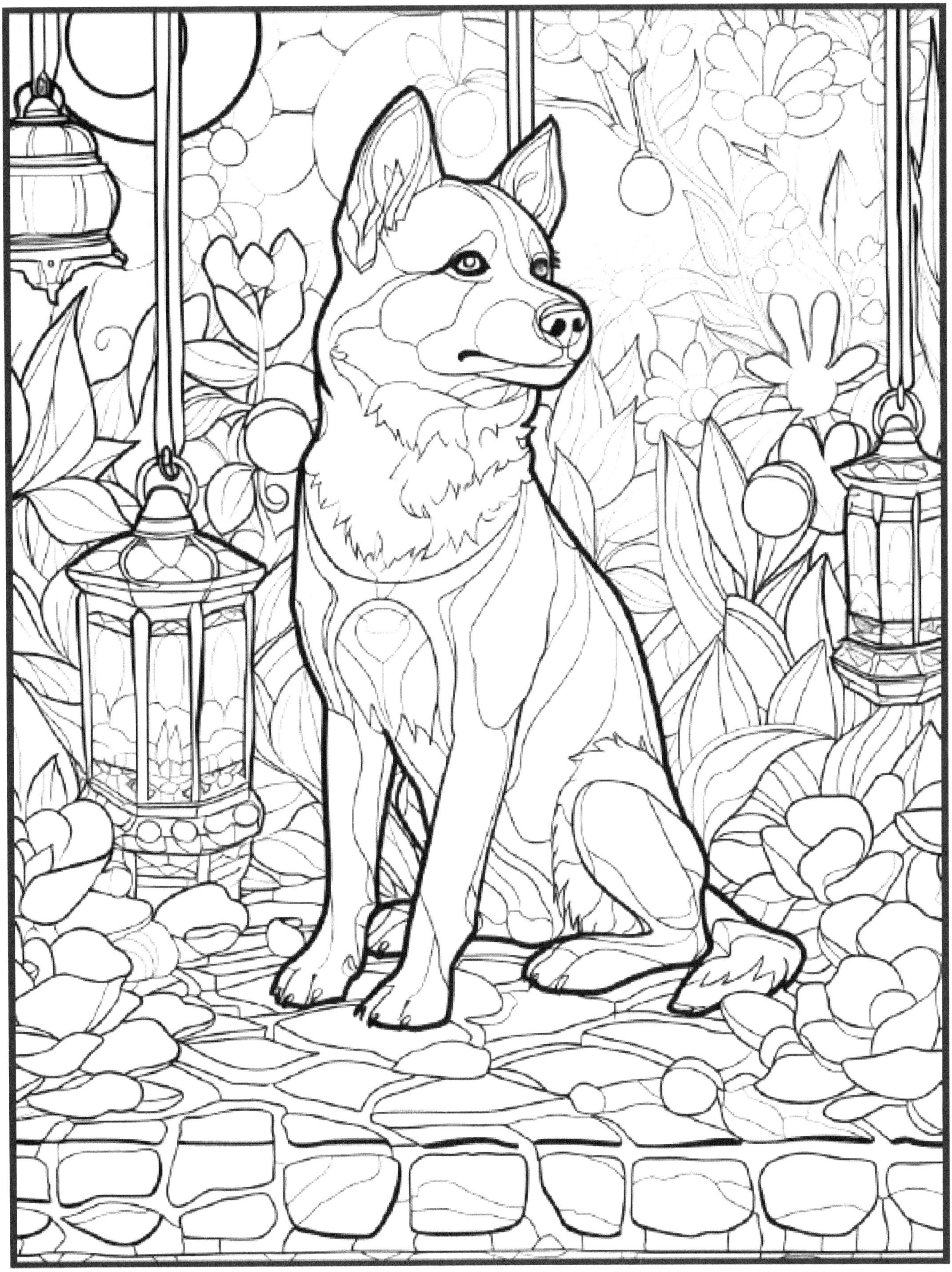

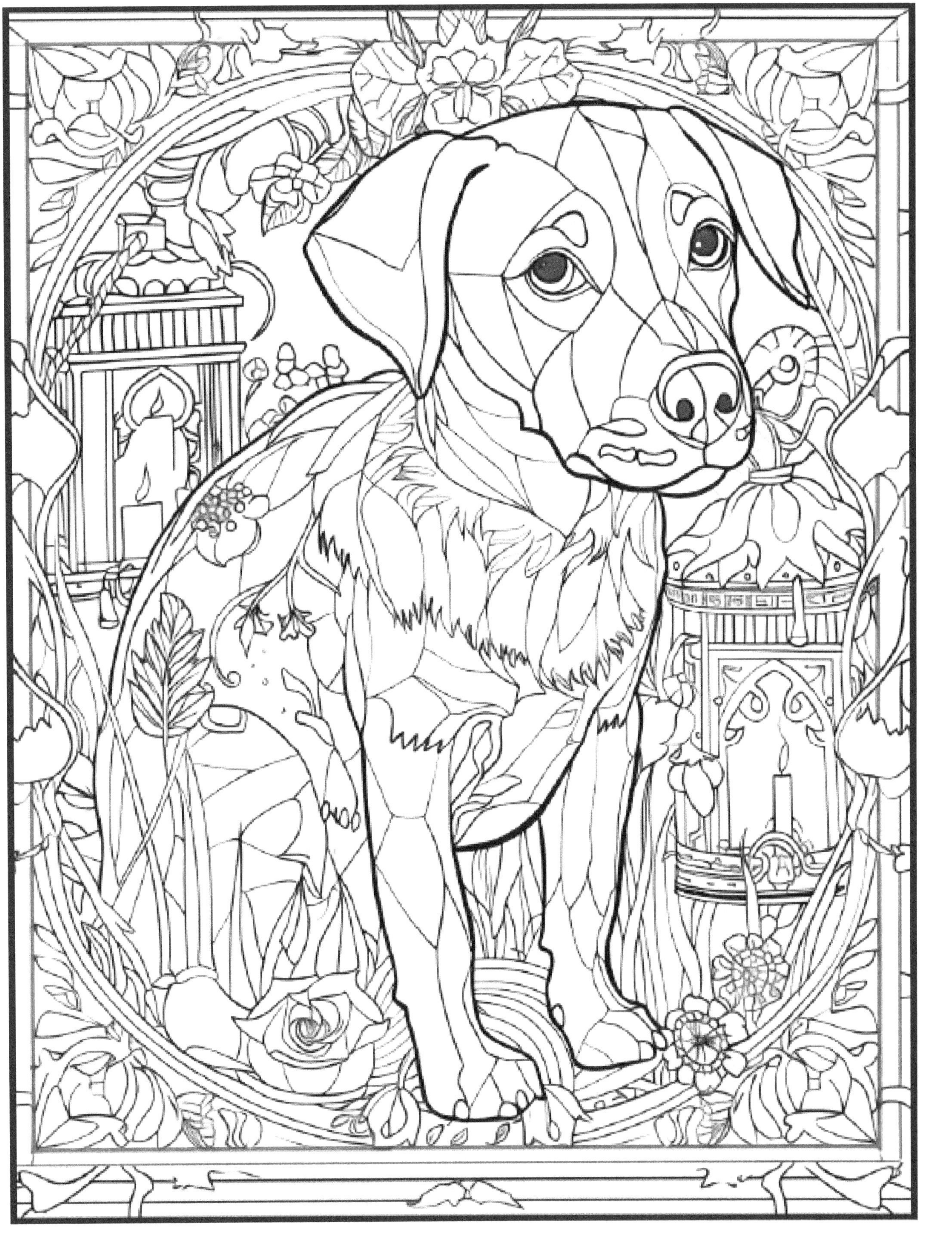

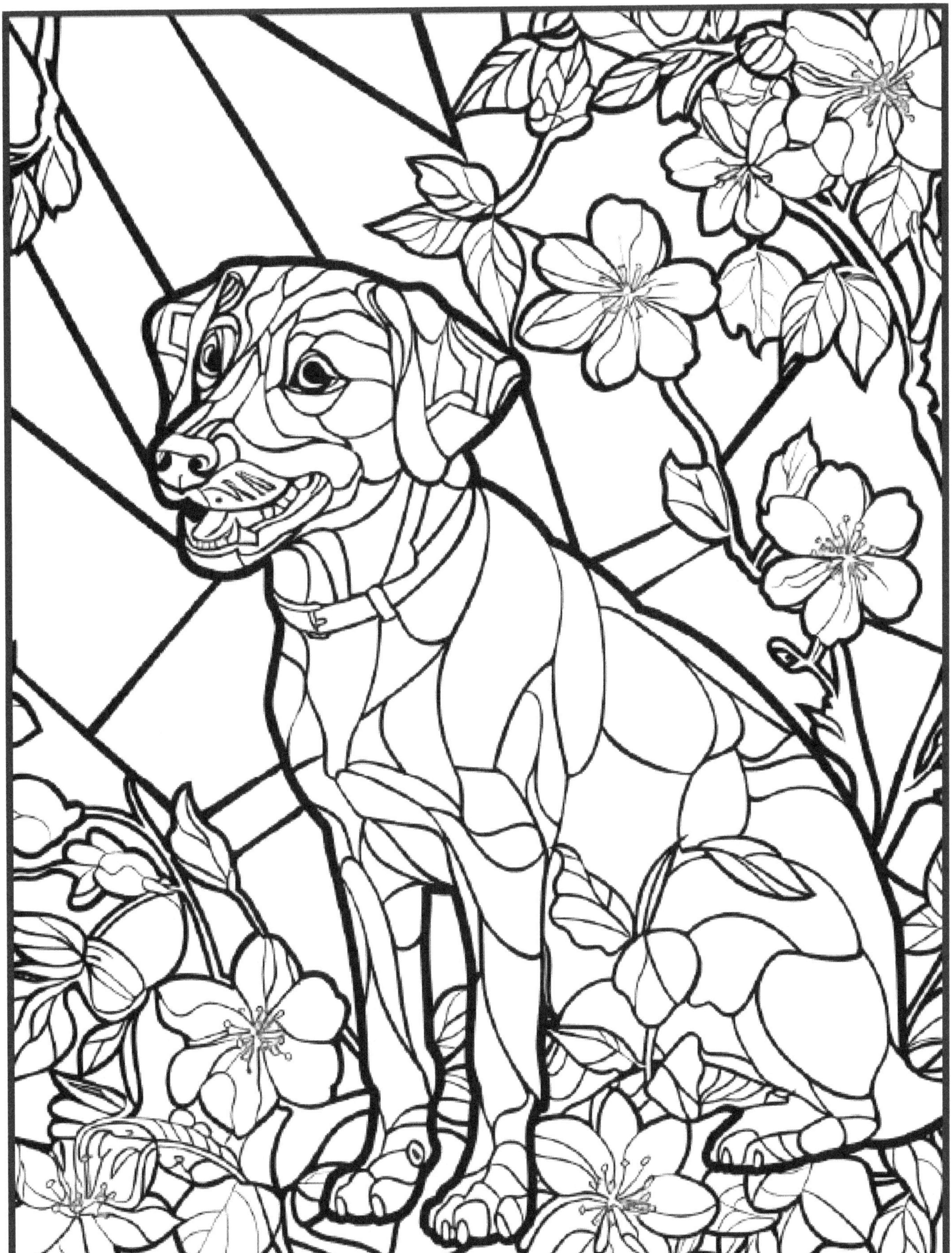

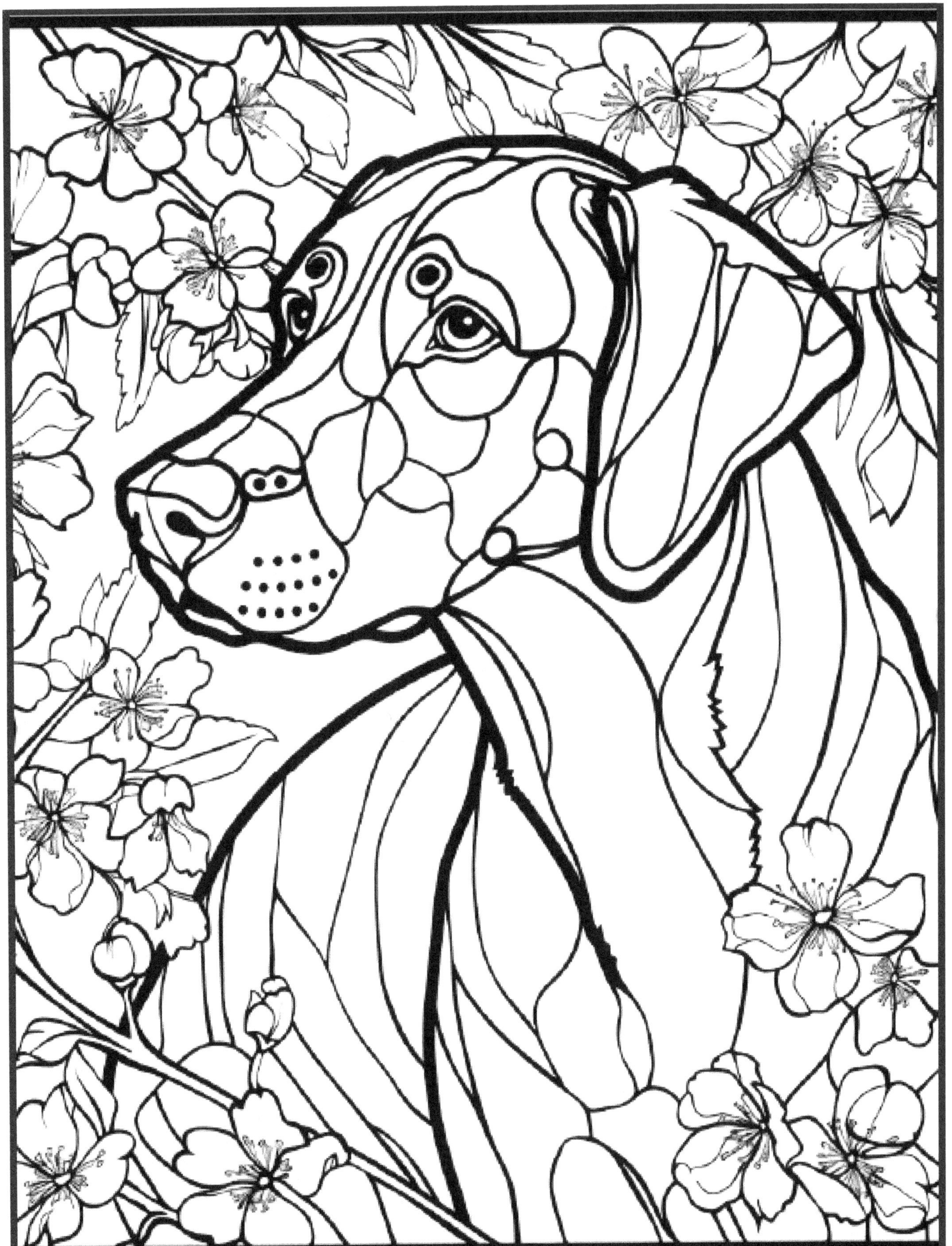

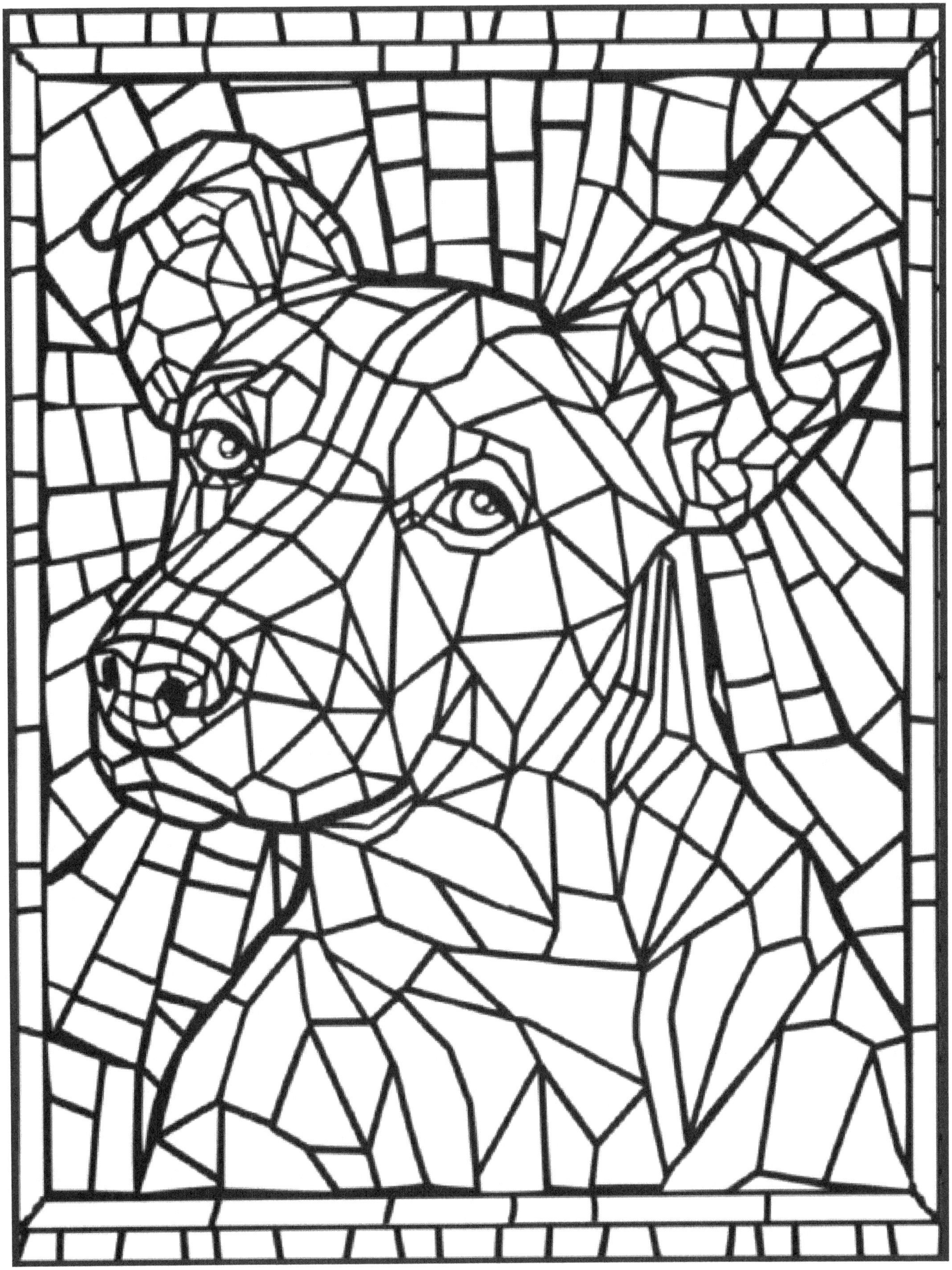

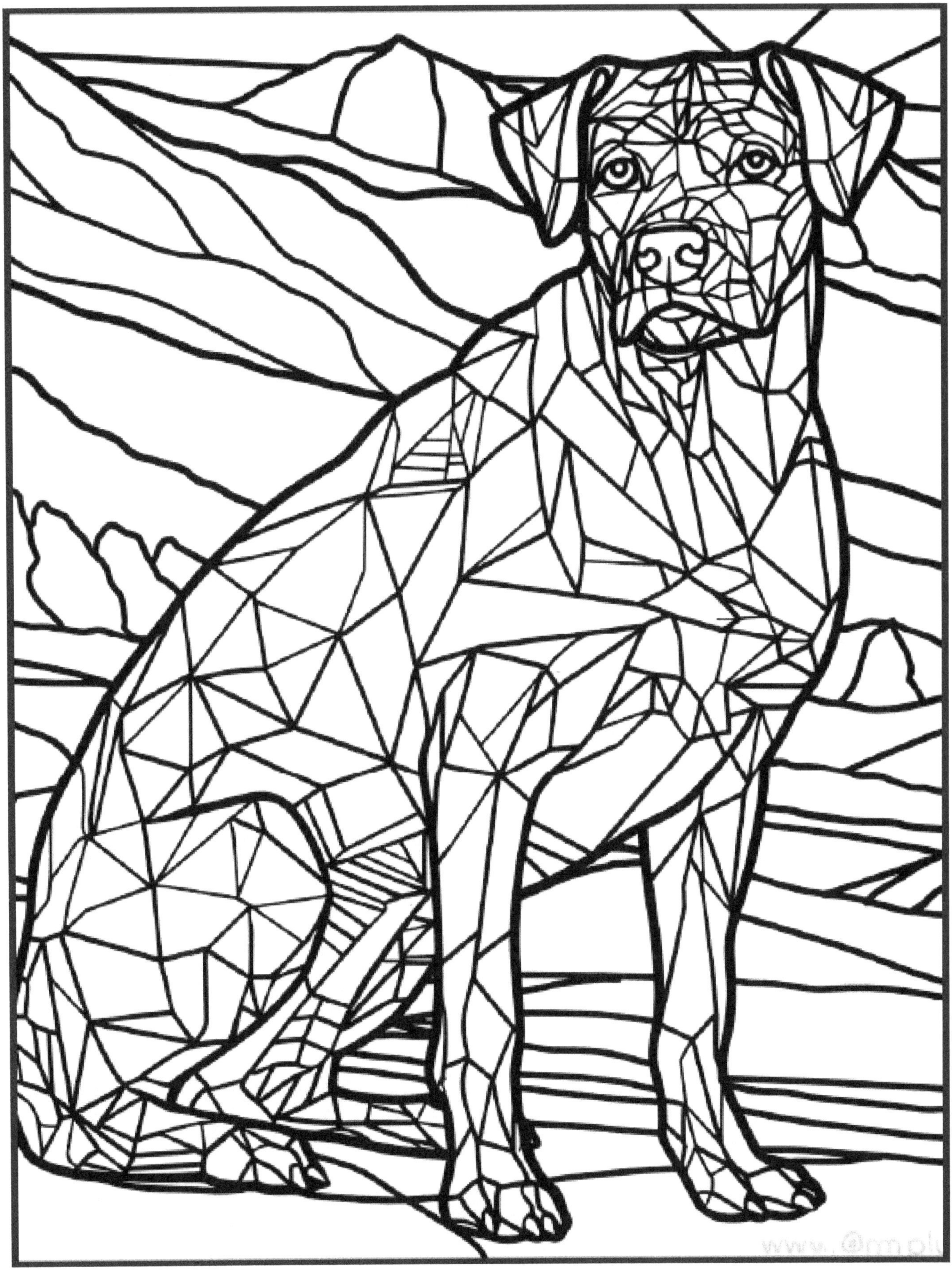

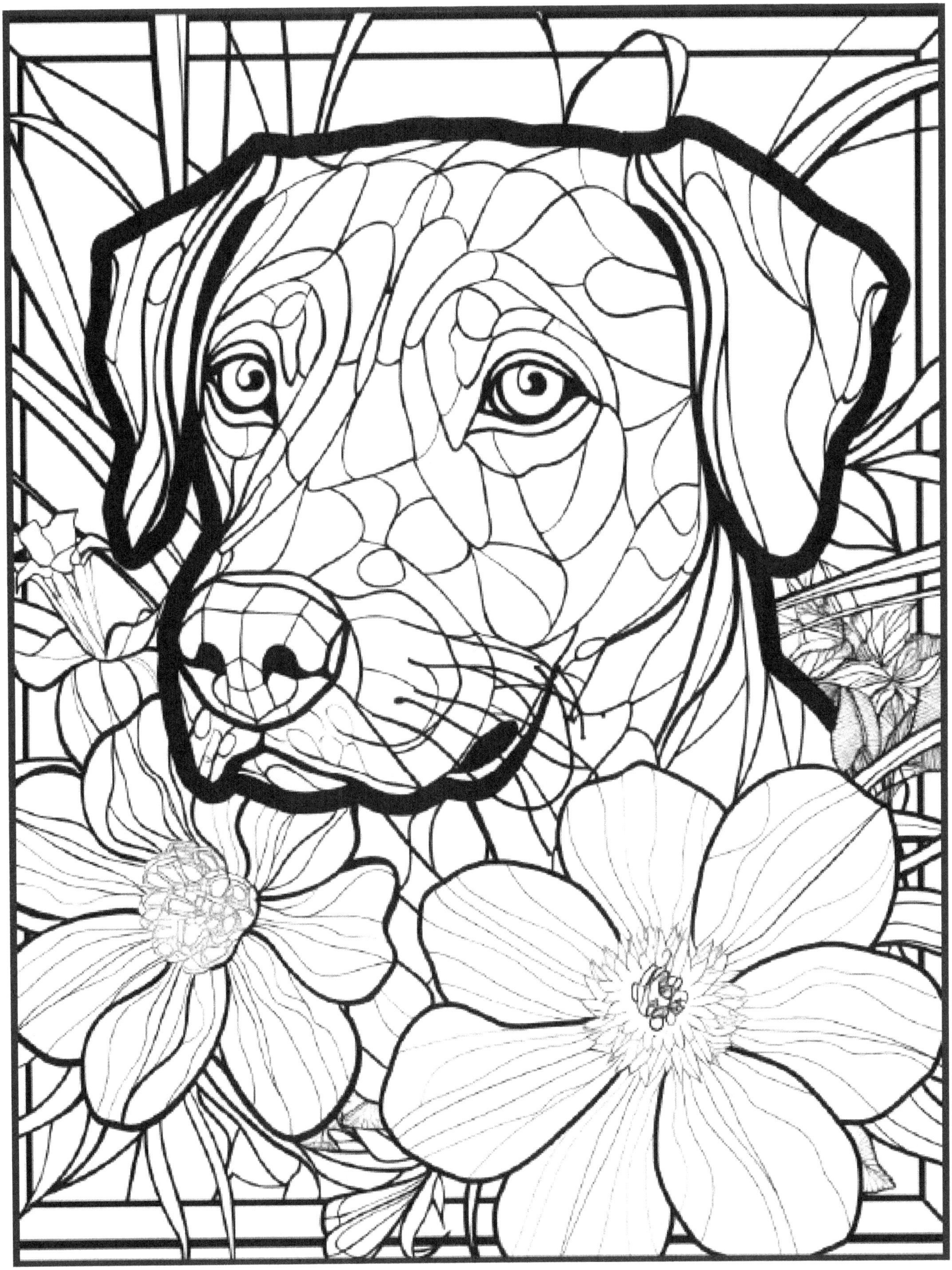

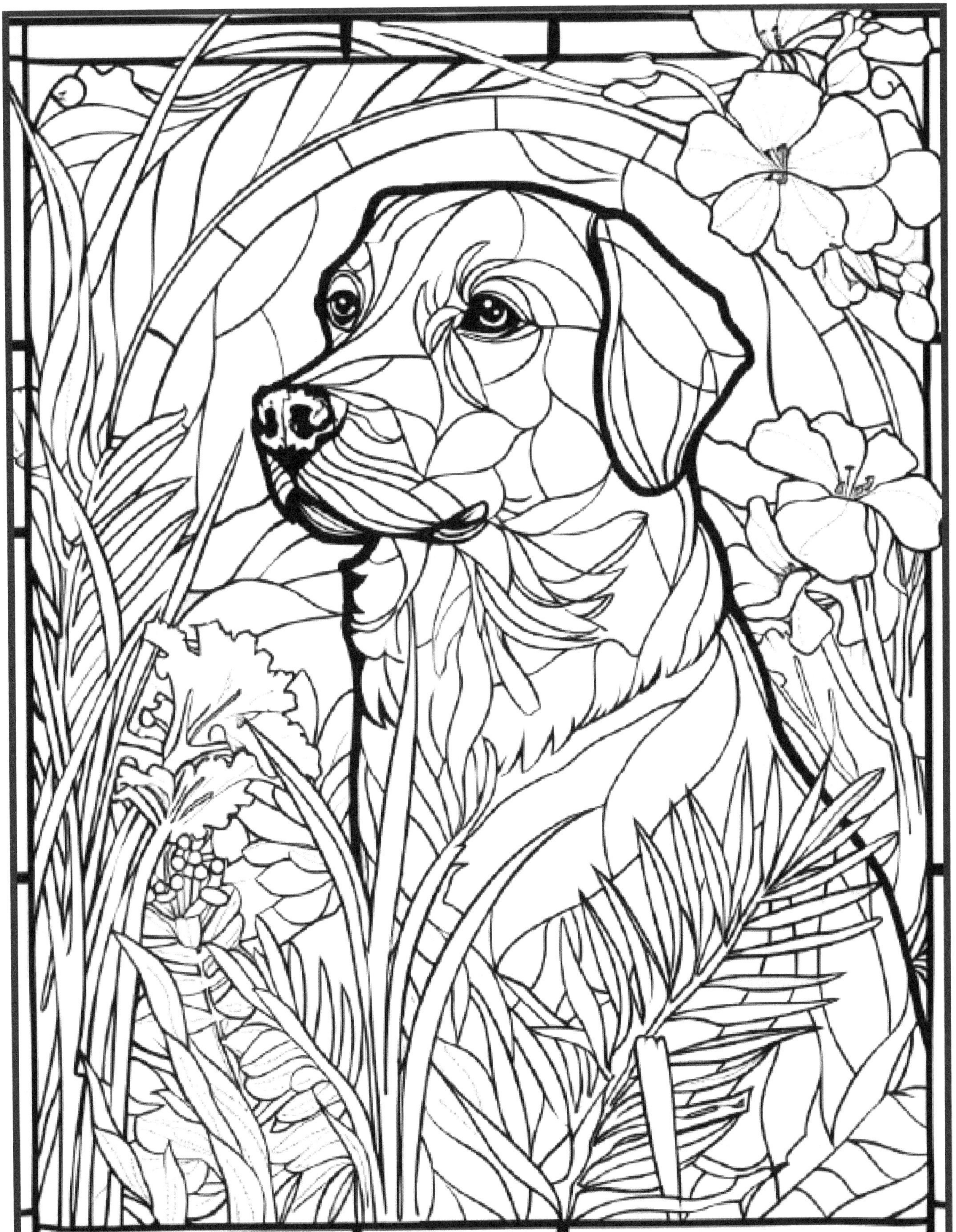

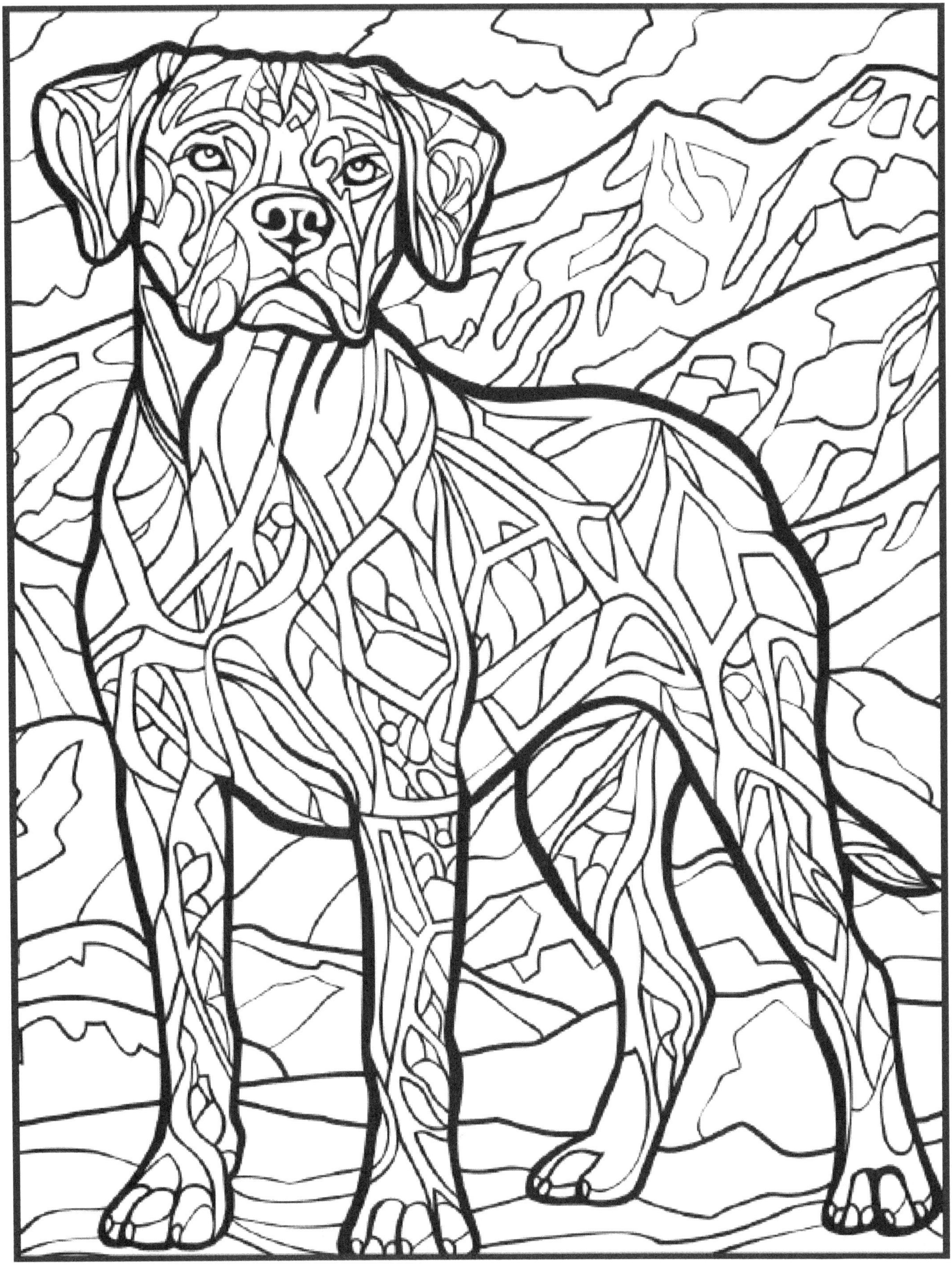

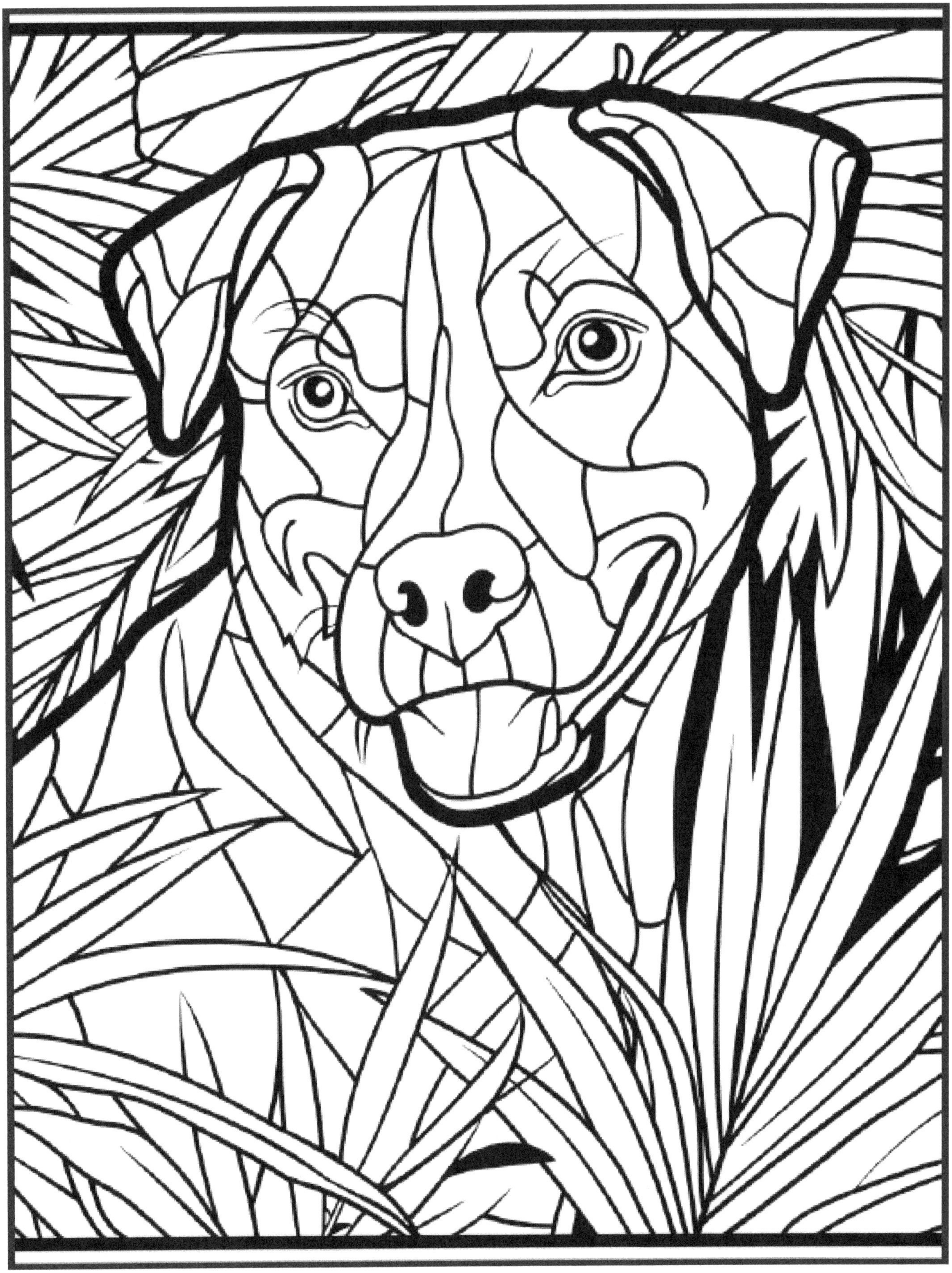

ColorQuest Collections

Fun and creative coloring books

Calming | Relaxing | Stress Relief

For more fun and creative coloring books, search for ColorQuest Collections in your favorite bookstore!

Copyright 2023. All rights reserved. No part of this book or this book as a whole may be used, reproduced, or transmitted in any form or means without written permission from the publisher.

www.ingramcontent.com/pod-product-compliance
Lightning Source LLC
Chambersburg PA
CBHW062113220526
45471CB00010B/3723
979832178 2767